NEGOTIATING WHILE BLACK

NEGOTIATING WHILE BLACK

Be Who You Are to Get What You Want

DAMALI PETERMAN

G. P. PUTNAM'S SONS
NEW YORK

PUTNAM
— EST. 1838 —
G. P. Putnam's Sons
Publishers Since 1838
An imprint of Penguin Random House LLC
penguinrandomhouse.com

Hardcover ISBN: 9780593544600
eBook ISBN: 9780593544617

Printed in the United States of America
1st Printing

This book is dedicated to my mother, Barbara, who always encourages me to be who I am to get what I want

This book is also dedicated to my sons, Chase and Cole, who continuously inspire me to do more to make the world a better place

Contents

Author's Note

I am honored that you are holding my book in your hands. I be
lieve that you—yes, YOU!—will find something in these pages
that will help you navigate your life more smoothly.

This book is definitely for a Black readership. It's also definitely
for a non-Black readership. How can these two things both be
true (I love a good paradox)? What this book is really about is
how to use your gifts regardless of your race, ethnicity, gender,
sexual orientation, job, and age (and the intersectionality of all of
the above!) to be the best negotiator you can be, even when the
odds are against you. If you have ever walked into a negotiation
and felt that there were other, unspoken factors at work, this book
is for you.

I bring to this book a wealth of knowledge derived both from
my personal and professional life. The stories are drawn from my
own experiences and the experiences of those whom I know and

have supported. In many cases, I have changed identifying details—such as names, pronouns, professions, locations, and/or the specifics of the conflicts—to protect the privacy of the individuals involved. I have gone to great lengths to disguise identities and recognizable details, sometimes creating composites from a variety of profiles. I carefully considered each change and found a balance between shielding characteristics and sharing relatable stories for you to connect with on a multitude of different levels. In other words, if you see yourself in or find yourself gravitating toward any of the stories that unfold in the following pages, please know that is both coincidental and intentional. It means my goal has been accomplished.

If you are holding this book, know that it is 100 percent written with YOU in mind. I wrote this book to challenge the notion that a one size fits all approach to negotiation works. The only constant in any negotiation is YOU. By the time you finish this book, you will have a toolkit full of easily implementable tools, greater awareness of your negotiation superpowers, some good stories to tell, and a few laughs along the way.

NEGOTIATING WHILE BLACK

PART I

The Basics

1.

Negotiation Isn't the Same for Everyone

Why One-Size-Fits-All Negotiation Fails

It happened again.

I needed to buy a new car and was prepared—and expected—to get the best deal possible. I had learned the secrets from top-selling negotiation books: William Ury and Roger Fisher told me I can "get to yes" by "getting past no," Alexandra Carter reminded me to "ask for more," and Chris Voss told me to "never split the difference," even giving me a specific script to use for my car-buying scenario. I'd completed an eight-week online Negotiation Mastery course at Harvard Business School. Plus, I had a successful career as a lawyer and a mediator, using my own hard-won negotiation skills day in and day out to get the best results for my clients. I walked into the dealership confident, informed, and excited. I knew what I wanted, I knew what price I needed, and I had the tools to succeed. What could go wrong?

Everything.

When the salesman quoted a too-high price, I mirrored Voss's tactical empathy strategy, pursed my lips, lowered my voice, and replied, "That sounds great, but I'm sorry I can't do that."

The salesman froze.

"OK," he said. And that was it. Nothing followed—no counter-offer, no further conversation. (And this was well before car short-ages and supply-chain issues caused by the global COVID-19 pandemic emboldened car dealers to stick to the manufacturer's suggested retail price because supply and demand was in their favor. Old-fashioned haggling over numbers was still the norm.) But he refused to negotiate with me. He wasn't even giving me a "Let me see what I can do" type of OK. It was just a resigned shrug.

It was the same shrug I saw him exchange with another sales-man when I walked in, as if he had drawn the short straw to have to attend to me. I was dressed quite nicely, but not over the top. I'd walked into the dealership that day ready to buy. What could he possibly be thinking? Why wouldn't he negotiate with me?

Wait. Did he actually believe that I couldn't *afford* this car? Voss's book didn't quite anticipate that scenario. So I persisted, feeding him the lines I had expected to hear from him.

"Why don't you talk to your manager and see what he can do," I suggested, "because I really like this car."

A few minutes later the nonplussed salesman came back with his offer: "My manager is feeling generous today. He's going to take off . . . $250."

Two hundred and fifty dollars off a new car? That's it? The shoes I was wearing that day cost more than that discount. Still following my script, I replied, "I'm happy your manager is in a generous mood today, but that isn't the price I had in mind. Is there anything else you can do?"

He did the obligatory walk to the back office and returned with a "That's the best we can do." There was no negotiation. No engagement. He never even asked me what I wanted to pay. Our conversation was over. With that, he let me, or rather *encouraged* me, to leave the lot empty handed. So I did.

As I thought about it later, I realized he had truly *believed* me when I said I couldn't meet his price. It was one of the most confusing conversations I'd ever had, and I have conducted negotiations everywhere from rainforests in Heredia, hostels in Vienna, and clothing manufacturers in Shanghai to markets in Accra, boardrooms in Mexico City, and universities in Ahmedabad. As CEO and founder of BreakthroughADR (Alternative Dispute Resolution), a global conflict resolution company, I find myself smack in the middle of conflict daily. I *know* how to negotiate. But somehow, when it came to this kind of real-world, everyday negotiation, I abandoned my instincts and followed someone else's script. Why didn't it work for me?

Because at the end of the day, when I step into a negotiation, there are different forces at work than there are for people like Chris Voss, Roger Fisher, William Ury, Alexandra Carter, and many of the other smart, accomplished, and well-respected voices in the negotiation space.

Of course this plan didn't work! Why? Because I was negotiating while Black. And as a woman. And as a young(ish!) person. And as a whole bunch of other characteristics that are specific to *me*. For as much wisdom and insight as those books offered, I was facing a kind of implicit bias that the scripts in the other negotiation books just didn't consider. Those strategies failed me because they didn't address the additional hurdle (or several) that I have to overcome before I can even show up as my authentic self at the negotiating table.

I needed a different game plan.

WHY ONE-SIZE-FITS-ALL NEGOTIATION FAILS

Of course, this isn't a situation that's unique to me. If you've ever gone into a car dealership—or sought to lease or buy a property, discussed your salary, or attempted to buy anything from a street vendor—and tried to negotiate with some standardized bag of tricks (only to come out with subpar results), you are not alone. And that's not just my opinion—it's been proven time and time again in various industries.

In a 1995 Yale University study, Professor Ian Ayres trained thirty-six participants—some Black, some white; some male, some female—to negotiate in a similar manner for a new car. They visited more than two hundred car dealerships in Chicago, armed with a script they had to recite as they negotiated with the salespeople to buy a vehicle. What do you think happened?

Across the board, Black and female buyers received higher initial offers . . . and the salespeople were less willing to budge on that number during negotiation. Ayres speculated that many salespeople were operating with a predetermined stereotype that Black people and women are less knowledgeable and are unskilled negotiators, so they would be more willing to say yes to a higher price—that is, if the dealers believed they could afford the car to begin with. The prospective buyers all used the same script, but the same script doesn't work for everyone . . . because negotiation is not the same for everyone.

That was my experience, too. The basic negotiation scripts I tried out that day in the car dealership fell flat when they came out of my mouth because those scripts were not written with me or people who look like me in mind. For instance, one popular book tells readers to adopt a "late-night FM DJ" voice during tense moments in a negotiation—in other words, to sound vulnerable and deferential, even in a high-stakes conversation. I can see how this approach might work for a white man, and perhaps *all* other men, because let's face it, this is a disarming, radically different approach than the blustering, brash negotiating stance that we are used to seeing in a patriarchal society. But for a woman, the late-night FM DJ voice risks sounding . . . well, seductive. For a Black woman, it risks feeding directly into stereotypes of the "oversexualized" jezebel. By speaking like this, I felt like I was putting myself in a precarious and weakened position. It wasn't me. And it just felt wrong.

Another popular negotiation book suggests using "negotiation jujitsu" to redirect positional statements and attacks against you. As the martial art in the technique's name implies, the authors tell you that when the person on the other side of the negotiation announces a firm position, criticizes you, and—wait for it—even attacks you, you are not supposed to engage. Rather, you should redirect. In theory, maybe that's valid. In practice, it equates to doing . . . nothing. The guidance in the book says do not push back, do not defend yourself, and do not counterattack. But here's the truth of the matter: marginalized people have never accomplished anything without pushing back, defending themselves, and strategically counterattacking with boycotts, marches, lobbying, and other methods. Lack of engagement in any context, to me, doesn't feel natural or authentic.

What if Black homeowners Paul Austin and Tenisha Tate-Austin had tried employing negotiation jujitsu when a real estate appraiser undervalued their home based on their race? In a widely covered story in early 2023, the Austins sought an appraisal of their Californian home to help them refinance their mortgage. When their appraisal came back well below market value, they were flabbergasted. Doing nothing would have cost them the opportunity to secure the loan for the upgrades they intended to make. "Not engaging" sounds great in theory, but in practice, negotiation jujitsu fails when there is bias embedded in the system. The Austins took a different approach.

Instead of employing negotiation jujitsu, Paul and Tenisha pushed back, and pushed back hard. They removed all family photos from the home and had a white family pretend that the house was theirs when the new appraiser came. The result? The new appraisal for their family home came in approximately $500,000 higher than their initial one—just as they knew it should.

You can't look behind positions if there is a smoke screen. You have to defend who you are and your ideas, especially when you are being gaslit.

You can't always assume that people are being genuine. You have to trust your instincts.

Negotiation advice has to reflect the multicultural society that we live in and suggest nuanced techniques that are applicable to everyone, *especially* those of us who were overlooked in prior negotiation books.

I don't know about you, but I was tired of following negotiation scripts that were not designed with me in mind. Wasn't there a way I could be authentically myself—a calm, funny, occasionally inappropriate, but always thoughtfully considerate woman—

and still negotiate effectively for myself, my family, and my clients?

I knew there could be. Because I do it every day.

I run my own global conflict resolution firm where, by providing training, mediation, and consulting, I help thousands of clients and individuals negotiate to get the results they want. I teach mediation at Howard University School of Law, I've served on the board of and as a trainer for New York Peace Institute, and I am a member of the President's Leadership Council for the international peace-building powerhouse Search for Common Ground. Over the years, I have been a part of negotiations that impact many aspects of your life—from the chips you eat, to the drinks you consume, to the beauty products you use, to the engine in your car, to your computer cloud storage, and to the electronics on your desk. I have even trained hundreds of New York City police officers to use their words instead of their weapons to de-escalate conflict. Negotiation is my life.

But get this: I don't negotiate or teach negotiations using the same old bag of tricks that we've always been taught. Heck, I probably don't use the same tricks that YOU do, even if you're also Black and female. In this book, you will get my playbook on how to negotiate in real life—if you're Black, yes, but also if you're simply someone who has realized that the cookie-cutter negotiation playbook doesn't work for you.

This book is for *everyone* and *anyone* who has been underestimated at the negotiating table, and for those who have tried the "traditional" pathways in bargaining and haven't found consistent success. There's a reason for that: you can't use a one-size-fits-all negotiation style when we are not one-size-fits-all people. People want to be seen as equal, but everything isn't equal. The only constant in every negotiation is *you*. This book prepares you to show up in the world ready to negotiate authentically as you. It turns out you can negotiate as yourself and win! I'll show you how.

YOU ARE THE CONSTANT IN ANY NEGOTIATION

As a Black woman, I've been underestimated at many negotiations, from boardrooms and bazaars to corporate offices and, yes, car dealerships. That's what's missing from most advice, which assumes that everyone is at the same starting line when you enter a negotiation and ignores the reality of racial bias, among other kinds of preconceptions. Regardless of preparation, skill, and education, for the Black, Indigenous, (and) People of Color (BIPOC) negotiator, there is always more at stake than deal terms. Not to mention the additional pressure you feel to do well because you want to keep the door open for others who look like you to have similar opportunities.

There are books on negotiation. There are books on gender. There are books on race. Where has the book been for people who face biases both blatant and implicit in negotiations every day? Why hasn't there been a book for people who feel like the plain-vanilla approach to negotiating did not or does not work for them? All the bestselling negotiation books on the market have solid, research-backed tips and varying degrees of success when used by white cisgender men (and perhaps some white women), but none of them scratch the surface when contemplating what a Black person is thinking and experiencing when they are negotiating.

From a bird's-eye view, this book is not about what makes us different. This book is about how as a whole we—Black people, people of color, women, and other people who check a box that makes them feel othered—have been excluded from the narrative when it comes to negotiating in real life. Until now, no one has attempted to explore the intersectionality of identity, bias, and negotiation while providing personal and professional skill-building tips in a book.

Before we go any further, I know that "Black identity" is not monolithic and that there is as much diversity within the African diaspora as there is outside it. I also know that not all people of color feel the same way, and to reference a quote that is commonly attributed in some variation to Zora Neale Hurston, Brackette Williams, and many black elders, "All skinfolk ain't kinfolk." Even within the Black community, we all have individual superpowers and snags. And for the record, I do not speak for all Black people everywhere, nor do I want to. I am also not speaking only to Black people in this book. I wrote this book for YOU, whether you are Black, white, Native, Latinx, Asian, Middle Eastern, female, male, or a member of the LGBTQIA+ family. Drawing on my decades of negotiation training and advising across different cultures, I have developed successful negotiation approaches that will help you become the best negotiator that you can be, while keeping in mind that the way that you show up in the world and your values and beliefs impact your negotiations.

This book is called *Negotiating While Black*, but it's really about how to use everything that makes you *YOU* to successfully negotiate any conflicts or opportunities that might come your way. Throughout, I will share with you lessons learned that you can apply to every type of negotiation imaginable. Each lesson will help you create your own tool kit with tried-and-true negotiation strategies to make your own.

NEGOTIATING IN REAL LIFE

This book is designed to be useful to you in your everyday life. Let's face it, most of us here aren't negotiating hostage releases or world peace daily. Instead, we're largely navigating everyday hurdles from mundane screen-time debates with a child, division of labor at home, and power dynamics within organizations to high-stakes business transactions and intense salary negotiations.

What we need is a practical book on how to negotiate in real life. You want to know how to succeed in a negotiation where no one else at the table looks like you. You want to know how to respond appropriately when you are in the grocery store and the person behind you rams you with their shopping cart and you have to quickly determine whether their strike was intentional.

And in the real world, you want to know how to face implicit and explicit bias.

ACKNOWLEDGING BIAS

Bias is often present in negotiation. Here are a few real-life scenarios to mull over. Can you name the type of bias in each?

- You have an employee twenty-plus years your junior who you micromanage because you don't believe the younger person has the experience, maturity, and judgment to make good decisions autonomously.

- A new opportunity to travel for work comes up in your department and you have two people who are qualified to take on the project. You offer the opportunity to the male employee without even discussing it with the female employee because she recently returned to the office from maternity leave. You don't think she will want to travel because she has a newborn.
- You are at a bar with some friends and an attractive person walks up to you and smiles. You were planning to head out, but you stay to chat with this person.
- You are at a networking event. You don't fully engage in any conversations until you know what the person does for a living, where they went to college, and what neighborhood they live in.
- You and your sibling are discussing care for your aging parent. Your sibling disregards all your suggestions because your sibling doesn't think that you are where you should be in your life, but your sibling checks all of society's boxes that define success.
- You approach a white male wearing scrubs in a hospital assuming that he is a doctor, but he's the physician's assistant and the doctor is the Black woman wearing scrubs sitting next to him.

As illustrated in these examples, a variety of different implicit biases appear in everyday situations. Common implicit biases that show up include affinity, ageism, attribution, beauty, education, gender, race/ethnicity, status, ability, ableism, and sexual orientation. And there is intersectionality that many don't even see or pick up on.

In this book we will not be dancing around the question of bias. Rather, I will be acknowledging its everyday existence and arming you with strategies for dealing with it.

ROAD MAP

Every great negotiation proceeds step-by-step. This book is organized to build your negotiation skills as you go, beginning with basic strategies and addressing a variety of situations where you must negotiate and resolve conflict in everyday life.

We start with some basic steps to empower you as a negotiator. In chapter 2, you'll learn, maybe to your surprise, that you already ARE a negotiator. You have all the skills you need, because *life* is a negotiation. Your advocacy for yourself and others means you already possess many of what I call the **Foundational Five** skills necessary for negotiation. In chapter 3, you'll learn how to come to any negotiation *just as you are*! I show you how to draw on your existing values and superpowers to bring your full self to the table, rather than tying yourself in knots pretending to be someone you aren't. In chapter 4, I show you how to learn more about the person you are negotiating with by peeking inside their bag. You'll learn how to research your counterpart, how to share yourself to learn more about others, and when sharing information is not the answer. Making the effort to understand where the other person is coming from pays off in ways both small and significant when it comes to your negotiations. In chapter 5, we discuss how to negotiate when either implicit or explicit bias is present. In chapter 6, you'll learn how to recover and repair rapport when an unintended offense occurs. In chapter 7, we discuss how to have "The Talk" with Black and brown people when dealing with law enforcement and how to navigate high-stakes negotiations. And in chapter 8, I will show you how not to get held back by common, triggering situations by learning to accept your emotions, and breaking through to the real you in order to protect your peace.

A NEW NEGOTIATION TOOL KIT

Back in the present day, I took all my hard-won experience about negotiating and overcoming bias with me as I drove to the next car dealership in search of a new vehicle. My first attempt at using someone else's playbook had been a bust. I thought to myself, *OK, now I am going to do this my way.*

Instead of playing the textbook role of a "good car negotiator," I showed up as me: a smart, funny Black woman who negotiates for a living. I'd done my research. I'd planned and practiced my approach. I knew I could roll with the unexpected if (when) it would arise. I was ready to get to work. My way of negotiating—what I call the Negotiation in Real Life (IRL) Tool Kit—involves, as a basic principle, establishing a rapport by not being afraid to show who I really am, while simultaneously acknowledging and hearing the other person.

The first thing I said (with a smile and an upbeat tone and cadence—abandoning that slow and sultry late-night FM DJ voice) when the salesman approached me was "Don't come over here unless you are ready to sell a car today." Caught a little off guard, he laughed immediately and escorted me over to his desk. If he had any initial implicit bias toward me, I wanted to interrupt it immediately by taking control of the conversation so that he could actually acknowledge me—Damali—not just a woman, not just a Black person, but *me*.

I wanted him to see me as witty, knowledgeable about cars, and prepared to leave the lot with the car—on my terms. I wanted to interrupt his bias and challenge any preconceived notions he may have had right from the beginning. My plan was first to make a connection and build a rapport with him. To do that, I had to learn a little bit more about him.

So, before he had a chance to talk shop, I asked him if he had grown up in the area or whether he had moved here as an adult. He paused for a moment and looked away from the computer, where he had been entering the specifications for my car, turning to me as if he were seeing me for the first time. He explained that he was from Manhattan and that his parents moved him to up-state New York when he was seven. In the ensuing conversation, he mentioned that he discovered his love for running track when he moved upstate. I immediately drew a parallel: one month prior, we had moved upstate from Manhattan with our two young sons, I explained.

"My oldest son should run track," I said. "He's only eight but he lives up to his name, Chase. I often wish I had given him a re-laxed name, because I have to run after him all the time. My youngest son's name is Cole. I got it right that time!" Throughout our chat, I continued trying to find our commonalities, not just because I'm a friendly and curious person but also because I know people are more willing to make a deal when they feel as if they have a connection to you, even if it's new.

Once common ground was reached and I'd gathered enough information, it was time to close. The salesman presented an offer, and because we had been able to establish that common ground, because we saw each other first as human beings and as equals, we were able to negotiate. Before long, I got the deal I wanted. And I got it *as myself* and on my terms.

In this book, I will help you do the same.

You'll learn all the tools I use and will soon be on your way to filling your own Negotiation IRL Tool Kit.

Let's go.

2.

The Foundational Five Elements of Every Negotiation

Why You're Probably Already Better at This Than You Think You Are

When I say the word "negotiate," it's like that scene in *The Lion King* when the hyenas shiver every time they hear the name "Mufasa." People react viscerally; they have some strong feelings about it. In the various trainings that I lead at my company, BreakthroughADR, I have asked thousands of people to tell me the first word that comes to their mind when I say "negotiation." Occasionally, people answer with positive words, such as "opportunity" and "chance." Usually, however, negative and highly emotionally charged words like "stress," "distress," "anger," "fight," "money," "debate," "struggle," "concession," and "fear" dominate the responses.

I'd like to change that. Negotiation shouldn't be seen as a negative thing or a stressful process. Rather, I want to normalize negotiations for you, because negotiations *are* normal. They are a part of everyday life. What does that mean?

Anything that you do that requires a decision to be made, an agreement to be reached, or a meeting of the minds is likely a negotiation.

- Not sure who will pick up the kids later? You have a quick chat with your spouse and you both recall all the things you have to do that day. By the end of that chat, you reach a joint decision that your spouse will pick up the kids because he has less on his plate than you do at pickup time. Decision made. Negotiation accomplished.
- Your new roommate seems nice, but he leaves dishes in the sink each night. Tired of seeing the disarray each day, you call out as you leave for class, "I will do the dishes each day if you take out the trash, OK?" Your roommate says, "Sure." Agreement reached. Successful negotiation complete.
- Your hairstylist feels like your hair needs "the works" when you come back from vacation. You say, "I need a deep conditioner (cost = twenty dollars), but I can do without the hair masque (cost = forty dollars)." She nods in resigned agreement as she holds your brittle hair. You just saved twenty dollars—and guess what? That short exchange, where you two reached an understanding, was a negotiation.

I am willing to bet that you go through the day effortlessly negotiating "the little things." You're probably not registering it because you are doing it naturally. You are T'Challa in the *Black Panther* movie, Shuri in the sequel, or Neo in the first *Matrix* movie when he dodged oncoming enemy gunfire by rearing backward. Each time that people, brands, stores, and internet ads present you with offers to "click here" or "buy this" or "watch this" or "start your free trial now," you negotiate a decision. When you check out in a store and the payment screen asks you whether you want to donate to a certain cause, you negotiate with yourself over how much to donate—or even at all. When you are having an internal dialogue to try to motivate yourself to go to the gym—that's a negotiation.

In all these examples, you aren't even in a discussion with another person—and that's OK. It's still a negotiation. We have internal negotiations with ourselves every day.

Negotiations are often defined as a *formal* discussion between people who are trying to reach an agreement, leading many people to believe negotiations are something that happens infrequently or only when the stakes are high, like in a prenup, salary discussion, or corporate merger. Yet most negotiations aren't formal. What makes a negotiation "formal," anyway—the presence of a table, high dollar amounts, someone wearing a top hat and bow tie? None of those things are prerequisites for a negotiation.

A negotiation is simply a discussion aimed at reaching an understanding, agreement, or decision. And all such discussions qualify, whether the two people are in dress suits or bathing suits. That "Mufasa" shiver you feel when you hear the word "negotiation"? It's usually unwarranted. Because news flash—negotiation is life.

YOU ARE A NEGOTIATOR
(AND YOU'RE PROBABLY BETTER THAN YOU THINK)

The level of discomfort some people feel around negotiations often extends to their perception of themselves as being bad at it. Again, I'd beg to differ. You are probably much better than you think. You might even be an absolutely gifted negotiator. You've just never thought of it that way before.

On a regular basis, many people, especially women and many women of color, tell me that they (1) are not negotiators, (2) never have the occasion to negotiate, or (3) do not know how to negotiate. If you fall into one of those three categories, let me ask you a few questions.

- Have you ever asked for something that you wanted?
- Did you know why you needed what you asked for?
- Did you communicate this want or need?
- Did you listen to hear how the person responded?
- Did you decide when the conversation was over?

If you answered "Yes," "Maybe," "I think so," or even "One time in band camp . . . ," you are a negotiator, you have negotiated, and you are probably better at it than you think.

Are you the person who is hesitant to go to bat for yourself or stand up for what you want, but the first person to advocate for a child, stranger, colleague, or even a dog? Then you are a negotiator! Sometimes it is easier, or more culturally acceptable, for someone to acknowledge their true negotiation skills when the recipient or beneficiary of their advocacy is someone else. Your skills negotiating for others, however, are skills that you can use to negotiate for yourself—you just don't realize it yet.

Take my mother, Barbara. She is kind, loving, and the most selfless person I have ever met. Everyone loves her right back: all the young Black men who live on our street take up a collection and buy her flowers for her birthday and Mother's Day every year because she has been a beacon of stability in the neighborhood during waves of gentrification. She considers herself to be shy (unless music is playing, and if so, you won't be able to get Barbara off the dance floor). She is also the classic conflict-avoidant person who will say "Never mind" or "I don't want it anymore" or "You can keep it" if challenged over something she wants. Barbara would be the first to tell you that she is not a negotiator and that she is uncomfortable negotiating. She'd rather sacrifice whatever benefit might be had than negotiate for herself.

The thing about Barbara, though, is that she has seven kids, and you better believe that she will advocate tirelessly for us. If we needed to be in an after-school program that was fully registered, my mother would make a call and we were in the program the next day. If we were being bullied at school or a teacher was not treating us fairly, my mother would appear in the principal's office the next day . . . and the day after that, and the day after *that*, until the situation was resolved.

Barbara may say she's not a negotiator, but when I was fourteen years old, I witnessed my mom do something that I thought was impossible: directly negotiate with the Washington, DC, government and win.

In the summer of 1993, I was eager to finally get my first summer job. Every day I checked the mailbox for the official letter from the DC Summer Youth Employment Program (SYEP), which would tell me my assignment. When it finally came, I was elated. I quickly ripped opened the letter. It said I'd been tasked with being a park attendant, working outside and cleaning the park each day. Summers in DC are brutally hot and humid, with the heat index often reaching 100°F (40°C), so it wasn't an ideal position, but I was stoked nonetheless—until I saw my mother's face when she read the letter.

"I'm going down there," she said.

Going where? I thought to myself. I mean, I thought it was awesome that my mom stayed home to raise us, but was she about to go to work with me on my new summer job? That might be a little much.

"To the SYEP office," she said.

"What? Why? I've been assigned my job. I know where to go and what time to report," I said.

"I am going there," she said, "if there was bias in the selection process, I want to negotiate a different job for you. I've heard several white people talk about their kids' summer jobs. They are all working in offices inside, with air-conditioning, in downtown DC. The DC government gave them the best jobs. You are a straight-A student, and while there isn't anything wrong with cleaning up the park, you deserve to have the same opportunities as those white kids."

I was stunned. It was my first official work assignment, and I had been thrilled. But my mother was born in the 1950s before the March on Washington for Jobs and Freedom in 1963. When she was in elementary school, schools were still being integrated, even though the pivotal 1954 US Supreme Court case *Brown v. Board of Education*, which ruled that segregation was unconstitutional, had been almost ten years earlier. To her, my summer job assignment was unjust and directly related to my race.

I pleaded with my mother, "Mom, it's OK. I can do this job. It's fine."

I recall being afraid that if my mom was unsuccessful, I would lose my place in the SYEP and possibly wind up with no job at all. Or what if I ended up with a job even worse for me, like picking up cicadas? (I was deathly afraid of all bugs until I confronted my fear directly by living in the rainforest in Costa Rica for eighteen months when I was twenty-six years old.) It hadn't occurred to me at age fourteen that there was a third option: that my mother would not leave the SYEP office until she had obtained the BEST job for me. A job that would change the course of my life and result in me starting not one but two companies over twenty years later.

Well, my mother went down there, and when she came back, I had a new job. Through SYEP, she'd enrolled me in a course on entrepreneurship at George Washington University. I was stunned. I was going to get paid to take a class at a college? It was my dream job. Thanks, SYEP! Thanks, Mom!

My mom rarely negotiated for herself, but she easily could have. We'll get into the details later of what she did right in her negotiations with SYEP, but for now, please know that anyone who could get me paid to take an entrepreneurship class at a prestigious university rather than being a park attendant during the brutally hot DC summer is not only a terrific mother—she is a negotiation shark.

My guess is that my mother is not alone in underplaying her skills and that you have people you have advocated for just like my mother advocated for me. Whom did you speak up for? Who needed something that YOU made happen for them? Did it happen at home, work, school, or some random place? Just think about the past week for a moment. Did your fifth grader need to switch a cocurricular class and you made it happen by writing to the school? Did your coworker ask you to cover for them so that they could take a day off and you approached your boss together to tell her how it would work? Did you see a stranger get treated unfairly or experience bias in front of you and you came to their defense? You are a negotiator.

When you advocate for others, you are using skills that will help you in your negotiations for yourself. It may take a conscious effort, but I want you to challenge yourself to reorient and take on a can-do attitude. Why? Because like Barbara, you can be—no, *you are*—fearless and bold. You are a negotiator, and you negotiate every day, whether you are aware of it or not.

FIVE ELEMENTS IN EVERY NEGOTIATION

Hopefully by now you've gained more confidence that you can do this. You are already a good negotiator. You advocate for yourself every day, and you probably advocate for others, too—and even more easily. So how do you go from good to great?

Here are the five elements of every negotiation that skilled negotiators know how to navigate. I refer to them as the **Foundational Five**. If you haven't before, you will start to see the Foundational Five in some form or fashion in each negotiation. Once you know them, you too will know how to negotiate like a pro.

The Foundational Five are:

1. Know what you want.
2. Know what you need.
3. Know how to actively listen.
4. Know how to communicate.
5. Know when to close.

1. Know What You Want

In order to get what you want, you have to know *what* you want. Every day we make statements about what we want. *I want a raise. I want a new car. I want you to do your homework.*

Clarity about what you want is a valuable skill when it comes to negotiation. Just think about it: if you do not know what you want and are not able to identify your desired outcome, your negotiation will be all over the place. In other words, how would you know whether your wants are getting met if you don't know what they are?

In the story I related, my mother knew she wanted me to have the best summer job possible. Her precision about that want was an incalculable advantage in her negotiation with the SYEP office. Knowing her want made her a force: she wasn't going to stop until she secured the employment she thought I deserved.

In negotiation terms, we call knowing what you want a *position*. A position is what you want to happen.

Consider Amina: Amina was pretty high up on the food chain and had a director-level position when I met her. I'd been chosen as a mediator between her and the company she was working for, Company A. Amina believed that she had not received a raise and a promotion in the last two program cycles due to discrimination against her as a gay Black woman. She lawyered up and threatened to sue Company A in state court if they could not reach an agreement in private mediation. Amina was very clear on her wants: she told me she wanted a raise, promotion, and back pay.

The representatives for Company A—Jason, the CEO, and

Mary, the chief human resources officer—of course, had different wants. They wanted to set the record straight and to prove that there was a legitimate business reason for not promoting Amina that had nothing to do with her race and sexual orientation.

These are two clear wants, or positions. Amina wanted a promotion; the company didn't want to promote her. Their wants were not only clear but in direct conflict.

As we explore Amina's story, you'll see that often you need to go beyond wants to get to a positive resolution. But at least at the beginning, it's good to know your position.

Like most things in life, wants or positions can run the spectrum from conservative to aspirational. And, get this, sometimes you may not know exactly what it is that you want, and that's OK. Still, you need to start somewhere.

What do you want most in a negotiation you are currently facing?

If this is an employment matter, do you want:

A higher salary?

Better benefits?

A better separation agreement or severance package?

Better terms that impact your new employment
opportunities, such as limited noncompete and
nonsolicitation provisions?

Better work-life balance and/or flexibility?

More days off?

To have your employer pay for your education or allow you
to seek professional development?

If this is a personal matter, do you want:

> To amicably separate?
>
> To figure out caregiver roles and responsibilities (for
>   children or parents)?
>
> To solve a child's problem with a teacher or a school?
>
> To sell your family home?
>
> To challenge a will?
>
> To have a better relationship with your spouse?

Think hard about what you want. Then write it down. Putting what you want into writing can help you concretize it, gain more clarity on it, and make it real.

2. Know What You Need

There is often a difference between what you want and what you need. A want is a position. It's *what* you want to happen. The need is *why* you want it to happen. The negotiation term for this is "interest." Positions and interests are driving forces in every negotiation. For example, your position may be that you *want* a new car, but your interest, or *why* you want the car, is because you are considering a job in a city that is not on the train line. Your brain shortcuts to thinking you must have a new car. But really what you *need* is a reliable way to get to work. And there may be a solution to that need that is not the new car. Distinguishing between your wants and your needs helps you clarify your bottom line in any negotiation.

Here's an example in a dialogue between a supervisor and supervisee to show the difference between want and need.

Supervisor: You wanted to talk about switching to a different
group?

Supervisee: Yes, to the sales team.

Supervisor: We don't have an open position in sales.

Supervisee: I am looking to learn a new aspect of the
company.

Supervisor: Well, our company is in the process of
restructuring, and we are creating a new in-house
marketing division. I think your skill set would be a good
fit. Would you like to hear more about the marketing
position?

Supervisee: Yes, I'd love the opportunity to utilize my skills
in the marketing division.

In this example, the supervisee thinks she wants to work in sales. But the supervisor doesn't have any more openings in that department. The negotiation might have stopped there if both sides focused only on their positions (i.e., wants to be in sales vs. no open sales role). However, because the supervisee shared what she needed in addition to what she wanted, the supervisor was able to come up with a solution to meet her needs (i.e., identifying an opening in a newly created department that satisfied the supervisee's reason for wanting to switch departments in the first place). Understanding the need or the why behind what you want can reveal entirely new possibilities for negotiations, as we saw with our supervisee.

It's not always easy to know our needs. If you're having trouble figuring out what you need, it may be helpful to use a framework presented by psychologist Abraham Maslow. According to Maslow's hierarchy of needs, the universal needs that motivate individuals can be grouped into five categories:

1. Self-actualization—desire to become the most that one can be
2. Esteem—respect, self-esteem, status, recognition, strength, and freedom
3. Love and belonging—friendship, intimacy, family, sense of connection
4. Safety—personal security, employment, resources, health, and property
5. Physiological—air, water, food, shelter, clothing, and reproduction

Note that our needs, according to Maslow, form a pyramid-like shape. In other words, Maslow believed you must satisfy the bottom needs of the pyramid, the physiological needs, before you are able to address the next level's needs, such as safety. And that this is true for each succeeding layer of the pyramid. So first and foremost, we must secure water and food (physiological needs), and only after we've secured these basic elements of survival do we look for employment and health (safety needs). Similarly, we look for familial relationships and intimacy (love and belonging needs) before we worry about "higher" items like respect or status (esteem needs). Concerns about "being all you can be" (self-actualization needs) come last and only after all other needs have been met.

You may, of course, move up or down a level of the pyramid as events occur. For example, if a health condition is treated (safety needs), you may feel more ready to start a family (love and belonging needs) or focus on creating a legacy (esteem needs). We have all experienced different levels of need in our lifetime and moved up and down the pyramid accordingly.

One interesting thing I've observed in my years of mediating and negotiating is that people do not always realize what is driving them. To recognize and articulate your underlying needs requires self-awareness and introspection. I've even had people tell me they want a goal that represents their self-actualization, even when their basic needs for adequate food and shelter haven't yet been met.

This lack of self-awareness about your needs leads to conflict. For example, if you ask for an internship to satisfy your need for a job with higher status (esteem needs), which you should definitely do, but what you really need is to pay your electricity bill (safety needs), you are going to be angry when you are offered a minimal stipend. It's better to be clear up front about what you actually need (i.e., a living wage) and negotiate for that from the beginning.

In Amina's case, Amina wanted a raise and a promotion. When I dug deeper, however, I discovered Amina had a lot of competing needs. First, she told me she needed to take a stand and speak up for what she saw as an injustice to her and people who checked boxes other than white, male, and cisgender. To meet her need of justice, she wanted the company to agree to require diversity, equity, and inclusion training. Second, she told me she needed to earn more money because she was the primary breadwinner in her family. My ears perked up at the latter.

As noted, fundamental needs like food, shelter, security, and resources for one's family are lower on Maslow's hierarchy of needs than a promotion and the status that goes with it. If Amina's basic need for earning more was not satisfied, like our intern, she would stay angry and in conflict. Amina's need for additional income was her **Million-Dollar Need,** or the need that drove all her other needs.

The company had needs, too. Company A received a lot of its funding from grants. That funding would all but cease if they ended up with a lawsuit alleging discrimination in a post–George Floyd world where many other companies were trying to be allies. Their Million-Dollar Need was to protect the company's and the CEO's reputation. Jason, their CEO, took it quite personally that Amina believed that she had been subjected to the alleged treatment on his watch.

Once I realized that what Amina really needed was more money for her family, hence her desire for a promotion, I could see a way to resolve the issue with Company A. We'll explore the details shortly, but remember that Jason needed to resolve the matter in mediation and keep it out of court and the news, and Amina needed more income. Their shared interests—settle this in a way that was both quiet and benefited Amina's bottom line—were more aligned than their initial wants or positions had suggested.

Negotiating from needs, concerns, and interests will always bear more fruit than focusing on wants, desires, and positions. The former gives you more room for creativity, while the latter may have you stuck at an impasse.

Let's return to *your* want. Did you write it down? Can you think about *why* you want what you want? What's your need? Is there a more basic need that underlies it? And what's your Million-Dollar Need that drives all other needs?

If you know what you need, not just what you want, you are already a successful negotiator.

3. Know How to Actively Listen

It sounds simple, but one of a negotiator's greatest strengths is knowing how to listen. There are many reasons we don't listen. We don't listen because we are thinking about what we want to say next. We don't listen because we have different speaking styles. We don't listen because we listen through filters of our own values, beliefs, and preconceived notions. We don't listen because we are generally distracted or easily distractable. And if we are being honest, sometimes we don't listen simply because we don't like what we are hearing, or we don't like the person who is speaking.

Yet listening to others is a critical way to get the information you need in a negotiation.

More important than ordinary listening, however, is *actively* listening. Active listening is when you hear, absorb, and understand what the other person is communicating verbally and nonverbally and then you summarize and validate what the speaker said.

Active listening is observing the nonverbal

To understand what another person is communicating, you need to observe their nonverbal communication: to *gauge* what they *aren't* saying and to *observe* what they are showing you. Sometimes this means asking everyone to turn on their cameras when you are negotiating over video so you can see everyone's faces (and they can see yours). Or it might mean having that important conversation in person, not over text, email, or phone. Sometimes it just means using the technique of silence and quietly observing whether the other person is twisting their hands in nervousness or if their face is starting to redden in suppressed anger.

It is unwise to overinterpret nonverbal cues because they can and do vary across cultures—beware of cultural bias. For example, I learned while working with Japanese clients and during my time as a student at Nagoya University of Foreign Studies that Japanese negotiators nod frequently. In America, nodding is often associated with agreement. In Japan, however, a negotiator nodding does not indicate agreement, but rather they are nodding out of respect to show that they are listening. Misinterpreting this nonverbal cue could lead to some uncomfortable conversations if you think there was agreement and there was not.

Active listening is a process where you need to use *all* your senses. The nonverbal clues you pick up on will be invaluable when it comes to knowing how to approach communication with the person you're negotiating with.

Validate, validate, validate!

When someone is in conflict, they feel disconnected and unheard. When paired with a good listener, by contrast, they feel more connected and positive. Research shows that people interacting with a good listener report attitudes that are less extreme and more complex. In other words, there is more mutuality and less one-sidedness in the conversation. Good listening primes people for clearer, friendlier, and smarter negotiations.

How do you show someone that you are actively listening to them? Validation is a useful communication skill that can help the other person reconnect and feel heard and understood. And the best part about validating someone else is that you don't have to agree with what the person is saying.

When Amina told me how unjust she felt Company A had been in refusing to acknowledge her contributions, I immediately saw that this was far from a dispassionate subject for her. As in most cases when we feel badly treated, she was angry. I heard it in her voice and observed it in the way her face would redden, her jaw would clench, and her hands would shake whenever she talked about Jason's decision to deny her the raise and promotion. Even when she wasn't raising her voice, I could tell through active listening that she was feeling a great deal of emotion.

After I listened to her, I was careful not to take a position on who was right or wrong in this situation. It's a mistake many people make. Many folks listen and then immediately express their opinion, judgment, or thoughts. Yet doing this is the opposite of validation. In fact, even though you may feel like you are being supportive and helping by expressing your opinion, you are not validating the person at all.

Validation is saying:

"That sounds really hard, Amina," and not "Jason mistreated
    you."
or
"I can see that this is taking a toll on you," and not "Bosses
    like Jason stink."

Reminder: You don't have to *agree* with someone's perspective to validate it. But you do need to show that you understand the other person's feelings and point of view.

How do you know that you are validating well? I use something that I call the **Understand Test.** If you can convey through validation that you understand the speaker without ever saying the words "I understand," then you are successfully validating.

Validation that passes the Understand Test is saying:

"It makes sense that you would be upset about that."
"I can see why you would think that."
"It tracks that you came to that conclusion."

And meaning it.

Validation is also a process of learning what someone is thinking and feeling. In order to do that, you may need to draw the other person out. A technique I used to learn more about Amina and Jason is called "Yes, and."

When I was an improvisational comedy student at the Upright Citizens Brigade, the "Yes, and" technique was a staple. It is when you accept what another person has said (that's the "yes") and then continue that line of thought (that's the "and").

For example:

Amina says: "Company A isn't giving me the raise I deserve."
You say: "Yes, and it sounds like they didn't plan for the raise in their budget this year."

The trick to "Yes, and" is to show you hear and understand what the other person is saying. You are not arguing with or contradicting them; you are merely adding additional avenues of thought. You know you are doing it wrong if you say:

"No."

"No, but . . ."

"OK, but . . ."

"Right, however . . ."

"Yes, and" is a gentle encouragement to get people to continue to say what they are saying. With Amina and Jason, I used it to validate what they were already telling me and asked them to tell me more until they assured me there was nothing more to share. Once we'd aired all their concerns, I could work with what they told me to help them best communicate their needs to the other side and find a mutual solution.

The goal of the "Yes, and" technique is to gather as much information as possible. I learned quite a bit using "Yes, and" with Amina and Jason.

Jason told me:

"I don't want to start a Company A precedent with what we decide today."

"No one else has brought these types of issues to our attention."

"We already approved the budget for the upcoming year. The raise isn't possible."

"We value Amina and want her to be happy. This may no longer be the place for her."

Jason's last statement was especially significant. When he suggested Company A might no longer be the place for Amina given her unhappiness, I knew that he was not looking to retain her and that a promotion that entailed Amina staying at the company was not in the cards.

Amina told me:

"I am willing to be a martyr for justice."

"I am not the first person at the company to feel this way."

"The raise is important to me, but it's the promotion in title that matters the most."

"I am ready to move on from this company."

Amina's last statement was the first clue I had that there might be another and better path to resolve her conflict with Company A.

Remember how my active listening told me how angry Amina was that she wasn't promoted? Active listening also told me when I was on track to a possible solution for her. As I validated her claims for justice, I noticed her jaw soften. Her breathing slow. She visibly relaxed. She then stated her readiness to move on from Company A so calmly and confidently I knew leaving Company A was a decision she had already thought about outside of our discussions. She was ready to go. On that, she and Jason agreed.

It was a short step from there to a potential solution. By using "Yes, and" to validate her further, I got the piece of information I needed that made all the puzzle pieces fall into place. Amina, it turned out, had already started exploring options beyond Company A for getting the salary and position she wanted. In the process, she'd discovered that to get the job she had her heart set on with her preferred salary, she needed to have a higher pay grade and title at her current job. Her desire for a promotion was really to (1) get the promotion and title upgrade at Company A, then

(2) leverage that to get a new job at Company B. My path to resolution was now clear: rather than help get her promoted at Company A, a route that would surely dead-end with Jason, I could help her make the job move she so clearly desired.

In my mediation with Company A and Amina, I did a lot of active listening and validating to get the conversation started—and to steer it in a fruitful direction. As mediator, I had an advantage. Because the mediator is the intermediary, both sides can be more inclined to trust the mediator with their thoughts than they would trust each other. I had no fixed position or interests per se; I was there to listen.

You, too, can practice your active listening and validation skills to draw out the other party. And the more you listen and validate, the more you'll discover about the other party's thinking, leading to a quicker and better resolution for all involved.

4. Know How to Communicate

As you've probably gathered by now, good communication is an essential skill for a negotiator. My mother's ability to communicate that I was a top student and that I deserved a shot at a job that would advance me in my career rather than one that would not highlight my talents won me the summer assignment that changed my life. Good communication starts with the steps discussed: clarity on want and need and active listening. Why is being clear so essential to communication in a good negotiation? First of all, people are busy and have a lot on their minds. You are trying to capture and hold fleeting attention spans. Second, being clear leaves less room for misinterpretation. Third, your clarity gives the listener the opportunity to ask questions if they need more information. At the risk of sounding cliché, communication is a two-way street, and when you are clear, you are engaging your listener and inviting them to be an active participant in the conversation.

Here are two additional tips that will make you a great communicator.

Be concise

One of the best ways to be clear is to state your wants and needs as concisely as possible. Eliminate unnecessary language or information. Be intentional about your word choice. It may take editing and re-editing to boil it down to the essentials. But think about how much easier it is for you to respond, and often respond positively, if someone else's ask is concise and easy to understand.

Sometimes concision even results in the unexpected. When I was pregnant with my first son, I worked at Weil, Gotshal & Manges, LLP, a major international law firm. Back then, many women attorneys with young kids told me I had three options after maternity leave: to quit, to come back full time, or to come back part time. I didn't want to quit, because I loved working there, and I was just starting to hit my stride as a midlevel associate. I didn't want to work part time either, because women who were part time told me that they were doing 100 percent of the work but getting paid around 40 percent less. However, I was nervous about working full time in the office with a newborn at home. None of the available options worked for me.

So instead of accepting the status quo, I made a big ask. I wrote a concise, deeply considered email that quickly established "I'm coming back." I wanted to put their minds immediately at ease that I was returning after my child's birth and have them in a calm state before the ask. "I want to propose something I hope you will consider," I continued in my note. "I would like to work full time and work from home two days a week. I live five avenues from the office, I have hired a full-time nanny, and this option would allow me to take care of my family and continue to do my job most effectively. If you ever need me to come in for an urgent meeting, I will be there. I know this arrangement has never been done before, but I would love to work together to find a solution that pleases everyone."

I knew this was a big ask (this was pre-COVID days, mind you!). I also knew I had a solid reputation in my practice group— private equity and mergers and acquisitions. I had mentored many people, and I was active in recruiting and retention efforts. I felt confident that the cochairs of my practice group wanted me to return to the firm after maternity leave and would be willing to work with me.

By focusing on a concise, clear solution, I played into what I had hoped would be our shared interest to make this a win-win. Much to my surprise, they said yes to my six-sentence proposal. I told every female lawyer I knew, both within and outside New York, and they couldn't believe it. At the time, this arrangement in corporate departments at big law firms was unprecedented and unheard of. With my brief email, I set a precedent at my firm and provided a new option for people returning after parental leave. I established the same precedent when I was pregnant with my second son and working in-house at the office of general counsel at Deloitte. In both cases, a concise, clear ask helped change the seemingly unchangeable taboo against working from home as a new mother.

Be personable

Like negotiation, persuasion is an art, not a science. Personable communication comes down to a few things, all of which we have already discussed: active listening, validation, and being empathetic. If you want to up your game when it comes to being personable, here are three more techniques to consider: using someone's name, recalling details about them, and using appropriate, subtle touch.

My mom, Barbara, is a master of personable persuasion. That summer day in DC, she arrived at the SYEP office unannounced and without an appointment. Yet she confidently walked up to the lobby of the small, fluorescent-lit, wood-paneled room and asked to speak with a SYEP coordinator.

"Do you have an appointment?" asked the Black woman at the front desk.

"No," said my mother, "but I have an urgent and time-sensitive matter, Ms. . . . What is your name, ma'am?"

"Kelly Warren."

"OK. Ms. Warren, my parents are from South Carolina, and they raised me to call people by their last name and to say 'ma'am' and 'sir.' It's a sign of respect."

Ms. Warren smiled and nodded. "My parents raised me the same way," she said.

"Ms. Warren, I am here to have my daughter's job assignment changed. Do you know who can help me with this?"

"I can help you," said Ms. Warren.

"OK," my mom said, putting her hands gently on Ms. Warren's desk. "The job my daughter was assigned is not the right fit. Damali makes straight As and she's on the honor roll. She wants to be a teacher or a lawyer one day and she needs a job that will get her closer to those goals."

"Your daughter does sound very accomplished, but we don't have any other job assignments," Ms. Warren said.

"Well, there must be something that you can do," my mother said, persisting. "You said your parents raised you the same way and I know you'll understand this: I am getting the sense that my daughter was assigned this type of job because her name gave away that she is Black, Ms. Warren. I've talked to other parents who aren't Black, and they told me that their kids all have office jobs. Do you think that's right?"

"Hmm. There are no other job assignments, but I did just hear about these summer classes at George Washington University. Let's take a look at those, shall we?" Ms. Warren answered with a smile.

My mom invariably got what she wanted by being personable. At the SYEP office, my mom not only *asked for the coordinator's name*, she continued to use it throughout. Using someone's name in a negotiation is a powerful way to be personable because it shows respect, courtesy, and recognition. To quote American writer Dale Carnegie, "A person's name is to that person the sweetest and most important sound in any language."

You don't want to say their name in every sentence. Find a balance. You can say their name at the beginning of a sentence when you want to direct their attention to what you are about to say. For example, "Ms. Warren, I am here to have my daughter's job assignment changed." Or you can say their name at the end of a statement when you are trying to make a point. For example, "I am getting the sense that my daughter was assigned this type of job because her name gave away that she is Black, Ms. Warren."

My mom is also the master of *remembering details about others*. To recall details, you don't have to have a photographic memory. You just need to remember things that they have told you about the situation, themselves, or someone else, as my mother did when she referenced her and Ms. Warren's common upbringing. You can say something as vague as "Didn't you tell me something about a company in Holland?" or you can be more precise, such as "Didn't you tell me about wind turbines manufacturers in the Netherlands plant?" At a minimum, try to remember even a single word (e.g., "wind," "turbines," "the Netherlands," "Damali"). Whatever works.

For *using touch*, I want to be clear that I am not advising you to touch people. Rather, I mean using nonverbal communication to emphasize a point. Nodding to confirm that you are listening (not necessarily that you are agreeing). Placing your hand gently on the desk as my mother did, or on a document you are referencing.

Masters of persuasion like my mom are experts at convincing someone of an idea or course of action. They navigate that person to a predestined place that reflects the desired outcome by connecting with them and revealing options they hadn't initially considered. I persuade people all the time to see things my way or, at a minimum, a different way than they had initially intended.

5. Know When to Close

All good things must come to an end, and that includes your negotiation. You have to figure out when the discussion is over and what you need to feel confident that you have an agreement.

Knowing when to close means you get what you want and

there is a plan to give it to you. In Amina's case, once I had all the information in place, Jason agreed to give Amina her need: the title and higher pay grade from Company A that would allow her to successfully secure the job at Company B at the level she desired. Amina would be able to move to a company that would give her the money and security she wanted for her family. I saw this as a huge win for Amina. I'd addressed her fundamental want and need. Yet when I gave her the good news, Amina was initially resistant to close because it felt like a different answer to her asks. To her, it did not feel like apples to apples. It's like when you ask for five things and the person gives you one. It feels inequitable. That can happen. The close doesn't always come in the way you expect.

When it is unclear when to close, what do you do? In my experience, the top five reasons people don't know when to close are:

1. You may have unfulfilled wants or needs.
2. There were some surprises in the negotiation.
3. You need more time to think.
4. The right person was not at the table (e.g., maybe the person didn't have enough authority).
5. You have a better alternative solution.

Amina and Jason knew that it was time to close when the result of the negotiations met their shared interests. For Amina, that meant getting the title from Company A to move on to Company B. For Jason, that meant keeping Company A's and his reputation intact, while helping Amina leave the company amicably. Amina had not had all her asks met. Her demand for training for diversity, equity, and inclusion wasn't met. But she also knew that

Jason had learned a lesson in the process of the mediation and would strive to make Company A's outside rhetoric match its inner processes. Ultimately, she could live with this resolution.

There were no surprises in the negotiation that caught Amina and Jason off guard. When you are considering when to close, it is also important to measure against the efficiency of time. For example, you don't want to negotiate for a week to get a fifty-dollar reduction in a car price, but you might be committed to more protracted negotiations regarding job position, child custody, and so on. Having both Jason and Mary present during the negotiation was helpful, as they were the ultimate decisionmakers for Company A and had the authority to enter into an agreement with Amina. Neither Amina nor the company had an external better alternative to their resolution, what Fisher and Ury would call a "best alternative to a negotiated agreement," or BATNA. All BATNA means is, at the end of the day, if you don't reach an agreement with your counterparty, what are you going to do? It is important to measure what's being offered against the alternatives you may have other than what is being negotiated. For all intents and purposes, Amina and Jason were ready to close.

Knowing when to close is often a matter of trusting your instincts. A script can't give you every scenario, but here are some things you can consider for guidance about when you should walk away or close:

- Did I get what I wanted or needed?
- Did I get more than what I bargained for?
- Have I conceded more than I had planned to?
- Is a better alternative available to me?
- Is there anyone else I might bring the matter to?

- What do I gain/lose by spending more time on this?
- What do I risk if I continue to negotiate?

When you are ready to wrap, I suggest keeping it simple. When I am wrapping things up, I control the things that I can, namely, what I do (my behavior) and what I say (my choice of words).

Your behavior at closing is key. You don't want the other side to have buyer's remorse because you start gleefully moonwalking away from the table while they are preparing to sign on the dotted line. Essentially, you don't want to cast any doubt on your interaction or make them question your good faith. Conversely, you don't want to be too solemn because that will send the message that you are not happy with the resolution.

Your choice of words at closing is also important. Give the other side sound bites that they can share with their clients or whomever they report to. Help them control the narrative, save face, or socialize the resulting agreements with their side. Say things like, "I know this is more than you wanted to pay, but this decreases the exposure for your shareholders." Or "You put up a good fight." Or "I don't want to have to negotiate with you again!"

Sometimes, a handshake, a nod, or a smile is enough to provide finality and evoke confidence that all sides have a mutual understanding. Often, people want to have the agreed-upon terms memorialized in writing. Close on your own terms and get what you need before moving on.

Know what you want, know what you need, know how to actively listen, know how to communicate, and know when to close: that's it. Those are the Foundational Five. They are part of every nego-tiation. And as predicted earlier, I bet you've used all these skills and more daily, without even knowing that you were doing so. What I see, and what I have seen all along, is that you are a nego-tiator. And you *are* a negotiator . . . even if most of the negotiations you've done have been for others.

NEGOTIATION IRL TOOL KIT

- Remember the Foundational Five. To negotiate from a place of power, know what you want, know what you need, know how to actively listen, know how to communicate, and know when to close.
- Identify the Million-Dollar Need. Highlight the need that drives all other needs for you (and, if possible, for your counterpart).
- Use the Understand Test. Determine whether you are vali-dating someone correctly by summarizing what you hear so effectively that you convey that you understand them and how they feel without ever uttering the words "I understand."
- Use "Yes, and." Encourage someone to speak more so that you can gather more information.
- Be concise. State your wants and needs as clearly and suc-cinctly as possible.
- Be personable. Do this by saying the other person's name, re-calling details of what they have said, and using subtle and appropriate touch to underline a point.

3.

Show Them Who You Are

Why Their Perception of You Is Your Negotiating Superpower

An urgent text appeared on my phone. *"Can you talk now?"*

Leyla wasn't the type to text me in distress; something was definitely up. I called her and she answered on the first ring. In a whisper, she told me her boss had just fired her. She was still reeling from being caught off guard. And it got worse. She'd been "terminated without cause," so she hadn't done anything wrong. It wasn't like she'd sold company trade secrets or annoyed a client. Her boss told her that he was firing her because she "wasn't a good fit for the company."

Not a good fit? Leyla's pedigree is impeccable. Ivy League educated. Internationally trained. MBA. Prior work experience. She's the entire package, and—wait for it—Leyla is a female venture capitalist (VC)! According to a report published by Women in VC, a global community of women in venture capital with representation in more than sixty-five countries and over two hundred cities, women are significantly underrepresented in the profession, making up around 5 percent of venture capitalists. This percentage, though low, quadrupled over a five-year period due to targeted efforts to recruit more women and women of color. Still, women of color VCs are almost nonexistent. Only three individuals identified themselves as women of color at the time of the report. In the company that had hired her only six months prior, Leyla was the youngest member of the team, the only woman, and the only person of color. Again, Leyla's a unicorn.

I asked Leyla to tell me about her hiring process. That was the first negotiation that she had engaged in with the company, and I was looking for clues to what had gone wrong. You can probably picture that first interview. Leyla said all the right things. She made all the white men who interviewed her feel comfortable. She mimicked their style and cadence. Made the right jokes. Leyla was the person that she needed to be to get the job and to secure the gig.

But then, this same team who loved her in the interviews had a very different reaction when she showed up at work as her authentic self. Determined to bridge the funding gap that existed for women entrepreneurs, she recommended using the funds she managed to invest in women. She'd hoped for excitement at her novel yet still profit-driven investment strategies. Instead, she was met with resistance. Whenever she spoke up to expose her team's implicit biases against female entrepreneurs or to show inconsistencies in the way that they evaluated the risks associated with investing in white-male-owned businesses as opposed to minority-owned businesses, she was met with dismay. Every time she showed up in all her millennial, female, person of color glory, they were not receptive.

The problem, however, wasn't simply what was happening at work. Leyla was in trouble even before her first day. As I explained to her, if Leyla had been honest about who she was and what her wants and needs were during the hiring process, it wouldn't have changed the people who hired her, but she would have seen the signs that they were not on the same page. Leyla became a venture capitalist so that she could invest in more women. This company was not a place in which she could accomplish what she'd vowed to do.

In the days of yore, we were all advised to dress and play the part to get a seat at the table. *Once you are there, you can make a difference and hold the door open for people like you,* they said. *It is easier to make change from the inside,* they said. However, what you risk when you show up under the auspices of "be who I have to be to get the job" is that if the person you've presented is any different from how you are 51 percent of the time (a majority), then that will come back to bite you. You may never feel like you fit in. Plus, as my grandmother used to say, an act can last for only so long.

Interviews—just like so many parts of our lives—are negotiations. So is asking for a larger budget for your project. Or a raise. Or to switch departments. Or countless other interactions you'll have at work and in the rest of your life every single day. To become a great negotiator, whether you're vying for a job or seeking funding or exploring new career opportunities, you have to be your authentic self.

BE YOUR AUTHENTIC SELF

The old negotiation model wants you to think that the only way you can be successful is to imitate all the successful men who have negotiated hostage releases, peace treaties, and high-stakes business deals in the past. Following that model, an "ideal" negotiator profile often emerges. Let me paint him for you—white, male, cisgender, assertive, and traditional. He gets results, sure—by following the scripts, models, and game plans of other people who look and think quite a lot like him.

But the problem with the old model goes deeper than that. Even if that profile is altered slightly to accommodate more wide-ranging views or a different gender, it's still a "copy me" model. *This exact approach worked for me; it will work for you, too. Do what I did and recreate my success.* It's an approach that tries to make us all the same, rather than acknowledge the differences between us. And this "copy me" model is promoted in many, many aspects of our lives.

Recall your first day of class at the school your older sibling attended. The teacher loved your older brother and held him out as the model you should emulate. *Be like your brother.*

Recall your first day at a college you transferred to spring semester. A professor introduced you to Malika, a straight-A student who was assigned to show you how to excel. *Be like Malika.*

Recall your first day at work. Your supervisor connected you with Bob and said he would be your mentor. People like Bob. He's very successful at work. *Be like Bob.*

The problem with trying to be your brother, Malika, or Bob in a negotiation is that it means that you will not be *yourself.* When you do not show up as yourself, you cannot be authentic because something will be off. It will take longer to build trust and establish a rapport, and research shows that trust and authenticity are intertwined. Why? Because there *is* something off, maybe disingenuous, when we are not ourselves. Truthfulness and transparency, by contrast, engender trust.

This is true in the business world, too. Consumers crave authenticity. But why are certain brands seen as authentic and others not? In a paper on the concept of authenticity in marketing, professors from the University of California, Bocconi University, and Vrije Universiteit Amsterdam show how consumption experiences that people deem "authentic" involve judgments about accuracy, among other things, with "accuracy" meaning the consumers felt the seller was being transparent and reliable in their communications. We trust individuals who convey truthful, accurate information to us. Similarly, we perceive people as authentic and trustworthy when they are being honest with others—and true to themselves.

Another component of authenticity, according to the same research, is integrity, which the professors define as being intrinsically motivated while acting consistently. Other studies back up this link between integrity, authenticity, and trust. A successful brand like Ben & Jerry's, known for delicious ice cream, has from the beginning built its reputation as two aging hippies who communicate exactly who they are, including their commitment to social justice and causes like the environment, and who keep those commitments through the ups and downs of the business cycle. We trust a brand that communicates and sticks to its values, especially, by the way, when the message is accompanied by warmth and competence. We trust Ben & Jerry's and embrace the brand precisely because of the authenticity and integrity of its founders. Many brands turn to authenticity campaigns to build their brand equity. The same thing is true for you in negotiations.

When you are authentically you, when you are true to yourself and act with integrity, you are building equity—in you.

UNIQUELY YOU, UNIQUELY VALUABLE

When you show people who you are, you tell a unique story about yourself that engenders trust and faith in your value. Another way of saying this is that when you show people who you are, you communicate your **unique value proposition**. Unique value proposition, or UVP, is a business term that explains what you stand for, who you are as a person/company, the benefits you offer, and what makes you unique. You see companies doing this all the time to justify everything from their existence in the marketplace to their price points. In every negotiation, you have to know your UVP in order to get what you are asking for.

Whenever I learn I'm going to be negotiating a deal for a client, I start by asking them to tell me about themselves. I want to know their story, who they are, and what makes them unique. Only then can I start to think creatively about matching up their unique value to a company's or another individual's unique want. Your UVP is your major selling point.

Consider Matthew Cherry, a former National Football League player who created an animated short film about a Black father who has to style his daughter's hair for the first time. Cherry wanted the film to be a positive representation of Black fathers and to promote natural hair love among young people of color. When he came across several viral videos of men doing their daughters' hair online, he was inspired to make his own film about "hair love." Only problem is: Animated films require money. Lots of it.

Now, negotiating with financiers is never easy. And this was Matthew Cherry's first animated short. But he had a story that reflected his values, his commitments, and things that were meaningful to him—Black representation in animated film and normalizing Black hair at home and in the workplace. Matthew was determined to succeed—and to use his UVP to do so.

Matthew also had a plan. As we'll discuss, we don't necessarily show everything about ourselves to everyone all the time. Rather, developing a UVP means thinking through what you are trying to communicate about who you are in a negotiation, identifying your target or whom you are communicating and negotiating with, and then developing a plan that reflects the steps you intend to take to connect your UVP to another's unique wants and needs so that you can achieve your goals.

First, Matthew made a deal for a children's book version of the story, so that he owned and controlled his intellectual property. That book eventually became a bestseller. Then, in 2017, he created a Kickstarter online campaign to raise the funds for the short film. He told his personal story and showed all the videos and illustrations of the Black fathers styling their children's hair, and the hair love came pouring back to him. Almost five thousand people ended up pledging a total of $284,000. As Karen Rupert Toliver, a longtime animation studio executive, said when she came on board: "There's never been a project that hit me so personally as 'Hair Love.' Living with Black hair my whole life, growing up in Texas . . . ," said Toliver. "The project really just spoke to me personally. And I was like, 'It has to get done.'"

The film did indeed get done. And in 2020, it showed in theaters nationwide before *The Angry Birds Movie 2*. The mother was voiced by Issa Rae of *Insecure*. And it had attracted the support and backing of celebrities from *Empire*'s Gabourey Sidibe to Gabrielle Union. The best news of all: it was nominated and eventually won the Oscar for Best Animated Short Film.

As for Matthew Cherry, by showing the world who he was, he had negotiated one of the best deals of his life. The *Washington Post* reported that Cherry said, "Ultimately, it's just a numbers game, and you just have to continue doing the work. If you focus on how you're affecting the culture and you're affecting change, the awards and things like that will come in. Even if they don't come, you're still doing great work." By being his authentic self, by communicating his values of who he was with transparency, and by having a well-developed plan by which to accomplish the goal, Matthew Cherry was extremely successful.

DEVELOPING YOUR UNIQUE VALUE PROPOSITION

1. **Tell your story**. You can tell it to another person. Or write it in a journal. Don't edit yourself. Just jot down some key anecdotes from your backstory or your life that help explain what makes you you. Try to think of the most meaningful and revealing moments you can.

2. **Define what makes you distinctive.** What's unique about you? Why are you the perfect person for the job or to solve a problem? What makes you stand out? What makes you or your company the perfect fit for this job/raise/investment?

3. **Identify your "target."** Whom are you negotiating with? Who is the audience for you/your product/your company? This could be the company you are trying to get a job at, the individuals or clients you are selling you or your product to, or the distributor for your wares. You are still you. That's the whole point of "show them who you are." But it can help you know what to emphasize as you discuss your unique strengths and qualities if you know whom your target audience is and what their wants and needs are as well.

4. **Consider what you stand for.** As we've discussed, integrity and communicating your commitments and values are an essential part of how you show people your authentic self. What do you stand for? What do you value? What intrinsically motivates you? Which causes do you embrace? Communicating and sticking to those values are important parts of your UVP.

5. **What's your plan?** How will you connect your UVP to another's unique needs and wants? What is your end goal? What are the steps you can take, showing who you are in each, to achieve it?

At each step, ask yourself what your goal was and whether you achieved it. Chances are that you did not achieve all of it, and therefore, you must ask the next question: What can you learn from this experience that will inform your follow-up or next task?

NORMALIZE TO CREATE A CONNECTION

Matthew Cherry is far from alone in using his story and the things that made him unique to create a unique value proposition. But often the creation of your UVP is not enough. You need others to recognize it and to meet you halfway. You need to connect your UVP to their UVP. This is where normalizing to create a connection comes in.

Dr. Rosemarie Ingleton, a.k.a. Dr. Rose, a board-certified dermatologist with over two decades of experience, was on the precipice of a deal with Sephora, a global skincare company and major manufacturer and distributor of cosmetics, when she first asked me to negotiate their contract. Dr. Rose had shown Sephora who she was, and Sephora liked what they saw. The only problem was that Sephora both did and didn't want the entirety of what she was offering. They wanted diverse cosmetics lines, especially ones run by successful practitioners and entrepreneurs. But they had some hesitancy in embracing the entirety of who Dr. Rose was and why she had created and brought her product to market in the first place. They had their model at the time, and frankly, her approach didn't entirely fit. Sephora had made their first steps toward giving Dr. Rose a chance to utilize their platform in a crowded retail skincare market. But they weren't champing at the bit to make many changes (if any) to their standard agreement. As the saying goes, from Sephora's perspective, "If it ain't broke, don't fix it." In order to get them to see why changes were necessary, I needed them to see Dr. Rose and her UVP, and make her story the norm, not the exception to the norm. I needed to normalize Sephora to Dr. Rose and to normalize Dr. Rose to them.

I asked Dr. Rose to start by telling me her story. Who was she? What was her unique backstory? How did it contribute to her UVP? She was eager to share it.

Dr. Rose had lived in Jamaica until she was sixteen years old, and those formative years there shaped her confident outlook on life. In her dermatology practice, Dr. Rose makes sure to show up as her full fabulous Jamaican self with every patient. She'd gotten into the cosmetics business after seeing a gap in the market for targeted skincare products for her patients. Dr. Rose believed that if Jamaican musicians Peter Tosh and Bob Marley could spread Jamaican music globally, she too could leave her mark by spreading her medical knowledge and the daily skincare routine of many Jamaicans to people all over the world. Each of her products features her trademarked "Jamaican Superfruit Blend," made of five fruit extracts native to Jamaica.

Taking an idea and bringing a product from concept to market involves many negotiations and, frankly, tests who you are and how you show up on a regular basis. When consulting with chemists to negotiate their engagement, Dr. Rose felt it was important that the chemists understood the Jamaican superfruits that she wanted to incorporate into her products, because she needed the right concentration to deliver on her brand promise. When she created her pitch deck to send to potential investors in the initial round of funding, she wanted to make sure that diverse models were included in the imagery so that her brand was staying true to all the beautiful shades of skin and ethnicities prominent on her island. Being authentic to who she was as a proud Jamaican woman served as an internal barometer for Dr. Rose.

We knew that Sephora wanted to sell products designed by industry experts like Dr. Rose. And that Dr. Rose's UVP matched their unique want. I needed to ensure that her value proposition was meeting their want head-on.

Normalizing is a standard technique in mediation. It is setting the parameters of what will be usual or standard in interactions with you. In many ways, normalizing is the opposite of "mirroring," or just repeating back to someone in a negotiation one to three words that they have said to you. When you normalize, you are looking to connect with someone. But in doing so, you aren't looking to parrot the other person. You are looking early on to establish your ways and feelings as the norm for you and then using that to find a meeting point or point of collaboration with someone else, all the while being respectful of *their* normal.

In Dr. Rose's case, I suggested that we use her story to help shape the negotiations and keep them on track. Whenever the negotiations would detour outside of who she was and what she wanted to show in her brand story, she needed to normalize who she was to the person on the other side of the table. Thus, when the marketing consultants told Dr. Rose that her marketing materials needed to make her brand accessible to all skin types, Dr. Rose understood that the marketing folks were trying to help her, but she pointed out that she was also the face of the brand, and the brand was named after her: "Rose Ingleton, MD." She agreed to use inclusive language in the print materials, because her products *are* designed for *all* skin tones, but she was also adamant that the imagery include tropical images from her island and people of color. That set the tone for not just the marketing campaign but all Dr. Rose's negotiations.

And by the way, normalizing goes both ways. I normalized Sephora to Dr. Rose, too. When we were negotiating, I normalized some of the terms and expectations that appeared in the contracts. I would say things like, "It is not unusual for companies to want to limit their risk," or "It is normal for companies to ask for assurances with respect to intellectual property."

Normalizing is important because it can feel like someone is taking a specific action that is personal to you, when really it's just an extension of what is normal to them or the way that they conduct business. I know this because I used to represent companies like Sephora in negotiations before shifting to help startups and emerging companies. Ultimately, my negotiations with Dr. Rose and Sephora were a success. And Dr. Rose's products have taken off: they are now available at Sephora, NET-A-PORTER, Saks Fifth Avenue, Neiman Marcus, Knockout Beauty, Revolve, and C.O. Bigelow Apothecaries. One of Dr. Rose's products even received what she calls the "Oscars of the beauty world"—coveted recognition by the Allure Best of Beauty 2022 Skin Care Awards in the Best Gel Facial Cleanser category.

As we've seen with both Matthew and Dr. Rose, there can be enormous success in creating your UVP and then normalizing your differences to create a connection. Do not hide your differences like Leyla. Show them who *you* are.

KNOW YOUR SUPERPOWERS

So how do we figure out who we really are and always lead with that person in negotiations? The first step in tapping into your authentic self is to find your positive attributes or the things that make you distinctive. You want to be *you* (not Bob!)—and specifically, you want to be the best version of you. You want to find your unique value proposition.

You also want to know your superpowers. Everyone has a special skill or two that helps them negotiate like a badass. For me, I never let the word "no"—or anything that *feels* like a no—stop me. People are always impressed by my ability to get what I want, regardless of the stakes. Want to know my secret? I'm an exceptional listener—that's my superpower. Some of my listening skills are learned, per the lessons in chapter 2; some are instinctual—I love listening to what someone else is telling me and trying to really understand where they're coming from. I've always been like that; it's something I was born with. Something that makes me distinctive.

Zahra, an Egyptian-born Muslim woman living in California, also has a particular set of superpowers. Zahra observes Ramadan, which is the holy month devoted to introspection, being thankful for what you have, considering those less fortunate, and being closer to Allah (the Islamic word for "God"). During this holy month, Zahra and other practicing Muslims fast from dawn to dusk. Dominant culture often sees Islam's monthlong fasting as something that has no secular value, but Zahra's faith and her ability to fast for thirty days from sunup to sundown are a source of Zahra's UVP—and her superpowers. Zahra is special because if she says she will do something, she does it. And that kind of consistency and follow-through makes her stand out. Zahra owns properties, subsidized by the state, that are devoted to housing low-income residents. Often, she has to engage in negotiations with the state so that she is paid regularly and on time. In Zahra's real-life negotiations, her superpowers of grit, steadfastness, and determination are significant assets.

Or consider Yael, born in Peru, living her best life in London at the helm of her financial services company. Yael's superpower is her fearlessness. She took what some would consider to be the rigid, buttoned-up, plain-vanilla field of accounting (I say this with love; I handled accounts payables in the accounting department of the Monterey Marriott for two years when I was getting my master's degree) and made her CFO services fun and less stressful for her clients by showing up as herself—a financial shark, down to the green hair. Yael rejects conformity to dominant culture norms and is authentically herself in each client interview and every negotiation. Her boldness particularly appeals to the LGBTQ+ audience, whom she helps to feel seen and heard in each negotiation. Her brand promise is to help her clients become financially free, fierce, and fearless with their money, and step one to doing that is showing what that looks like through her own example.

My listening skills, Yael's fearlessness, and Zahra's grit, steadfastness, and determination are but a few superpowers that help you rock at negotiations. Other superpowers, which may or may not be tied to one's full identity, include patience and flexibility.

Patience is an often highly underrecognized superpower when it comes to negotiation. Take Margaux, who was negotiating her salary for a new job. Margaux had rejected an offer of $120,000 and countered with $135,000. She had objective criteria on her side; she knew the salary range for the position was between $115,000 and $135,000. Basically, Margaux was sending the message with her counteroffer that she thought her education and experience supported her being at the top of the range. Margaux made her counteroffer on a Friday, and a week went by. Other people might have started freaking out. I've even had impatient clients want to negotiate against themselves (a cardinal no-no in negotiations) by offering to tell their employers to forget the higher number or conceding some other point solely because they started to worry prematurely. But Margaux was cool and composed. She knew the lapse in time might be due to the decisionmaker being unavailable, her contact being busy or sick, or any other legitimate purpose that had nothing to do with the thinking about her counteroffer. Patience was her superpower, and she was ready to wait. The following Monday, the company accepted Margaux's counteroffer.

Flexibility is another superpower—in negotiation and life. Khalid wanted to engage Oliver to build a new website for his company. Khalid wanted the works, but time was not on his side. He was planning to attend a conference in a week and wanted to put his new website on his business cards. Oliver told him that he could create a website for him, but that he needed more lead time to incorporate "the works." Khalid realized that he needed to be flexible. He and Oliver decided that a reasonable goal for the conference was to create just a landing page with the pertinent information and a photo of Khalid, so that when people searched for his company, they would at least see a website with his bio and contact info, even if it said "more coming soon." Khalid's superpower was flexibility, with a sprinkling of creative thinking.

Your superpower will probably not be my superpower or Zahra's, Yael's, Margaux's, or Khalid's. We possess lots of abilities—and every great negotiation doesn't have to use every single one. But knowing what you're good at—and how to leverage that to get what you need in a situation—is going to elevate your chances of success and increase your UVP.

Here are some questions to ask yourself as you think about your own superpowers: Are you a good listener? Are you steadfast, or do you have grit? Are you fearless? Are you exceptionally patient or flexible? Are you creative, and if so, in what way? What are you better at than anyone else who does your job? And how does that relate to your ask, or how might it be utilized in your negotiations? How might any of the above superpowers—or others—come together in stating your unique value proposition?

DON'T BE AFRAID TO REFRAME

A common response I get when I tell people to show others who they are is, *But wait, I am more than one person!* It's true. We are all multifaceted human beings. And we have more than one identity. Due to the intersectionality of our identities, we may show up as different people in different scenarios. At my kids' school, I may want to be the nice, approachable mom. While at work, I might want to be the skillfully shrewd negotiator or lawyer. And at my improv shows (yes, I do improv!), I want to be the funny, irreverent comedienne. Years ago, I took a conflict coaching course with Dr. Tricia Jones, and she said, "Identity shapes the kinds of power we use and are comfortable with." In other words, your intersectionality, in fact, can be another one of your superpowers! The trick is to understand how you want to be perceived and to frame or reframe others' perceptions accordingly.

You Can Frame—and Reframe—How People Perceive You

To show people who you are in a negotiation, you have to decide how you want to be perceived in the situation. This is often an ongoing inquiry. At any stage of a negotiation—before, during, and after—you can ask yourself two questions:

1. How do I want to be perceived?
2. How am I being perceived?

Jones and her coauthor, Ross Brinkert, say that our identities can be described in six categories: personal, professional, situational, relationship, organizational, and cultural. The authors challenge you to rank the importance of the aforementioned six identities to you in the situation by giving each one a rank of 1 to 6.

Consider each situation that you are in, and decide which categories apply to you: In this instance, am I Mom and thus acting with my mom priorities? Am I Jenny from the Block, trying to make others feel at ease? Am I the lawyer with expertise I want to demonstrate to others? Am I a combination of all these things? Only you can decide. You have control over your self-presentation. You can frame how others are perceiving you. And you can reframe it, according to a specific situation. So though I may be happy for my colleagues to perceive me as the time-minding, efficient negotiator, I may want my kids to understand that I always have time for them and their problems.

Reframing should not be confused with inauthenticity. Research shows that we cannot possibly adhere to one true self or a prevailing identity. Professor Herminia Ibarra calls this the authenticity paradox. Ibarra focuses on how three problems arise when one adheres to a rigid definition of authenticity. First, staying true to yourself is tough when we are constantly evolving with experience. Also, as mentioned earlier, different situations call for different versions of ourselves to lead. Second, finding balance between what we think, say, and do can be challenging because if you share too much, as we will explore in the next section, you risk your credibility and effectiveness. And third, leading with values from past experiences can be helpful, as we have seen in the case of Zahra, but may have limitations when used to solve a new obstacle.

So what do you do? Psychologist Dan McAdams, who has devoted his career to analyzing the psychology of life stories, says our stories constantly evolve. Knowing this feels like the antidote to the negative self-talk of when we tell ourselves that we are code-switching or when we experience self-imposed impostor syndrome. We are not being fake or inauthentic when we allow another aspect of our identities to take a front seat or a back seat if that is what the negotiation calls for.

It's interesting to apply this understanding to someone like Leyla, our female VC. As I mentioned at the beginning of this chapter, I would have advised her to test the waters with her full self in her initial job interviews. If she'd then picked up the signals that there was resistance, she'd need to make a decision: Did she want her identity as a supporter of women's businesses to be in the front seat or back seat of this particular job and negotiation? It might have been authentic of her to decide that her plan was to be Bob in this job, learn the company's ropes, and then use the skills she'd picked up there to move on to work at a more female-supportive investment firm—or even to start her own. It's fine to frame—and reframe—who you are. And to let your story evolve as you develop and actualize your unique value proposition. Or she might have walked away from the get-go. Only she could say what was inauthentic and what was true to her in that situation.

SHARE WHO YOU ARE, BUT APPROPRIATELY

In some negotiations, it may not be appropriate to share every-thing about yourself. I want you to consider three questions when you are trying to determine what is appropriate to share.

Is the information that you want to share relevant to the ne-gotiation in question? You have to ask yourself *why* you are shar-ing this information. For example, connect the share to why you applied for the job or why you entered this field. Leyla's desire to fund female entrepreneurs was absolutely relevant to her position as a VC, so in that case, I would have recommended her sharing that information. Dr. Rose knew her identity as a Jamaican skin-care expert was crucial to her product, that she wanted that reflected in her marketing, and that she wanted her models to reflect her Jamaican background. This, too, was relevant to her negotiation with the marketing team.

Does the information that you want to share add value to your position? Let's face it. There are some things that you may share that will add value to your position and some things that may be held against you (even if they are unaware of it or would deny it). Leyla's funding of companies that might otherwise go unnoticed by the VC world and yet could be highly profitable was absolutely something that could have added value to her em-ployer. Again, I would have recommended sharing that one of her goals at the company was to diversify her portfolio of funds with underrepresented entrepreneurs. This isn't to say Leyla should have shared everything. Remember how I mentioned that Leyla was a unicorn because she was a female VC? Something that Leyla might not want to share during the interview was that she did not plan to sleep until at least half of the people working in that VC firm were women or people of color. Why shouldn't she share that? Because that would mean that the people interviewing her (she was, after all, the first woman and person of color to be hired) would lose their jobs.

Would you feel like you are not being true to yourself if you didn't share it? If you are the type of person who enters every room and leads with your story, then the interview should be no different. See how Dr. Rose approached her negotiations with Sephora. Leyla, by contrast, had some things she might have wanted to hold back. For example, she may not have wanted to share that she is a serial entrepreneur and that she started and dissolved fourteen companies within the past ten years. Why? What do you think?

Remember: You are the narrator of your story. Think about what story you want to tell, consider your audience, and present the information as a strength. You are sharing your unique value proposition, and as long as you remain authentic to your values and your truth, you are fine in not including everything.

SOMETIMES THE NEGATIVE IS *YOUR* POSITIVE

Before we leave the topic of "show them who you are," I'd like to emphasize one last point: to be truly authentic to yourself—and find the things you're proud of therein—you may need to reframe your version of what's a negative and what's a positive.

Here's something I've discovered: people often see their distinctive attributes as negative ones. Rather than seeing one-of-a-kind strengths as positives, we tend to diminish and undervalue them. This is especially true for folks from a nondominant culture. Ruby White Starr, a twenty-five-year leader against violence against women, defines the dominant culture in America as "'whiteness', speaking English as a primary language, and being male, Christian, physically able, economically resourced, and heterosexual. These attributes create the norms against which all other subgroups are compared and judged." As a result, some of us keenly feel our lack of participation in the dominant group and the way we fall short of those norms. Before Matthew Cherry's film, many dads weren't even willing to talk about dealing with natural hair. And it's no mystery why. So many of us are programmed to do and say things to fit in and to steer clear from things that may make us stand out.

But guess what? It is what makes us different that makes us special. That's not just a *Sesame Street* slogan or a feel-good mantra. It's good, practical business sense—and embracing what makes you distinct in an environment makes you a savvy, talented negotiator. It's those aspects of who we are and how we move through the world that for so long we have been compelled or told to hide that are, in fact, the source of our power. My sense is that this happens more often than not to people who check a box.

Take Shirley, who pivoted midcareer. A former fishery biologist, she decided to attend law school at age fifty-three. She was concerned that when companies and government agencies started their recruiting efforts, she would not receive consideration because she was not the typical candidate due to her age.

"I am not who people expect to see when they come for on-campus interviews. I am older than a lot of my interviewers. I hope they can see how much I love the law and how much experience I bring to the table," Shirley explained.

Guess what? Her age and experience ended up being what her state's attorney general office, where she was hired out of law school, loved about her. The attorney general's office told Shirley that her experience was impressive and that she was exactly the type of attorney they were looking for because her background showed a commitment to public service. In fact, Shirley went on to represent the state's department of ecology in human and environmental health matters, utilizing her knowledge from her previous decades of work as a fishery biologist. And she worked as an assistant attorney general for the state for fifteen years from graduation through retirement. She thought that age would be a deterrent as she embarked on her legal career, but it worked in her favor because the people with whom she negotiates often assume that she's been practicing law a lot longer than she has. When her counterparts learn that she graduated from law school in the early 2000s, they are often shocked and then impressed.

Shirley turned what could have been a disadvantage into an advantage. She challenged the societal and business norms that make a departure from age or status quo feel like negatives and leaned into her difference, with a positive outcome.

Sometimes leaning into our differences not only turns a negative into a positive; it can even be an opportunity for change. I learned this firsthand through an experience with my son. In April 2022, my then ten-year-old son Chase told me that he wanted to lock (or "loc") his hair. Locking hair describes when your hair is coiled, braided, twisted, or palm-rolled to create a ropelike appearance. As a Black woman, I was excited that he chose this hairstyle. I didn't know Matthew Cherry's book or film back then. But as with many other Black people, I was hugely proud that he wanted a hairstyle so connected to our identity.

But as a mom, I was also scared. The world at large has not always accepted our beloved Black hairstyles, a lack of acceptance that has often bordered on the draconian and unduly harsh. I was keenly aware of examples of students who tried to stand out with their hair and in return had been severely sanctioned.

In 2018, high school student Andrew Johnson was given about ninety seconds to decide whether he would cut his locks on the spot or forfeit his wrestling match. Given that Andrew was already on the floor, competing, he chose to cut his locks. He was publicly humiliated in the process as images of a white female referee cutting his locks in front of the entire auditorium went viral on social media.

In 2019, high school student DeAndre Arnold was similarly banned by the school district from attending his graduation because of his lock hairstyle.

The issue in the situations of Andrew and DeAndre, and other instances where Black hairstyles have been censured or led to termination of employment, was that most Black hair in its natural state does not conform to Eurocentric beauty standards. The not-so-subliminal message from the dominant culture here is that to fit in or to be considered appropriate or professional, Black people must straighten or chemically process their hair. In both of those instances, the boys wearing the hairstyles they preferred led to a conflict where they stood to lose what they had worked so hard to achieve. For Andrew, it was not being able to compete in a wrestling meet that he had trained for. For DeAndre, it was not being able to participate in his high school graduation.

Yet these two boys' humiliating experiences and the outrage that followed also helped change the national conversation over Black hair. As I've said, sometimes the negative is actually a positive. And sometimes the recognition of that leads to change. The punitive treatment of Andrew and DeAndre, who were simply being who they were, led other Black Americans to bring the boys' unfair treatment to the attention of the government. The result was the development of the CROWN Act. CROWN stands for "Creating a Respectful and Open World for Natural Hair." At this time, twenty-two states (and over forty municipalities) have enacted the CROWN Act or similar legislation, and over twenty other states have prefiled, filed, or intend to introduce the legislation. I've also since learned that in 2020 DeAndre joined Matthew Cherry for the Oscar ceremony for his award-winning short film, *Hair Love*. Sometimes life comes full circle.

DeAndre's and Andrew's life-altering experiences paved the way for my son to wear his hair with pride.

Even still, I was conflicted when it came to honoring Chase's desire to lock his hair. He was the only Black child in his grade level and one of a handful of Black students in the entire private school, so I was afraid his hairstyle would draw attention and potentially make him stand out more. I also knew my son was embracing his identity and loving himself and his hair, and I wanted to support him in showing others his authentic self.

Ultimately, I did not succumb to my fear. *Sometimes what at first looks like a negative is a positive*, I reminded myself. Instead, I put my energy into preparing my son, his school, and the world around him for this change in his look.

I had Chase read two books: *Crown: An Ode to the Fresh Cut* by Derrick Barnes and *Don't Touch My Hair!* by Sharee Miller. I talked to him about the importance of being confident in his decision to show his school who he was through his chosen hairstyle. To help him share his culture and to be proud of who he was, I reminded him of that scene in the first *Black Panther* movie in which T'Challa was losing in the physical fight that would result in the winner being named king. Seeing her son struggle, the queen yelled out, "Show them who you are!" T'Challa went on to win the fight and was named king of Wakanda.

I wanted to do my part to frame the way that other people perceived Chase's new look, too. I reached out to Chase's principal because he greets every student and welcomes them at the front door of the school each day. He was the first person whom my son would see when he debuted his new look, and I wanted that first encounter to strike the right tone and balance for my son.

I then reached out to Chase's teacher. I sent her a fourth-grade curriculum that I found online that was developed to address hair diversity in Jewish cultures. I also sent her a copy of *Don't Touch My Hair* that she could keep in the classroom.

Both the principal and the teacher were immediately on board.

As I write this chapter, my son is celebrating the first anniversary of having his locks. Thanks to the bravery of DeAndre and Andrew; the vision of Matthew; and the team of Black women leaders Esi Eggleston Bracey, Kelli Richardson Lawson, Orlena Nwokah Blanchard, and Adjoa B. Asamoah; US lawmakers; and many others who fought for the CROWN Act, a negative has been turned into a positive. Being authentic can open the door to others' authenticity, whether you are aware of it or not.

The first step in being a great negotiator is being aware of all the wonderful gifts that you bring to the table. You will never have to split the difference if you lean into your differences and see them

for the positive superpowers that they are. Once you fully understand yourself and your unique value proposition, you're ready to
take the next step in mastering negotiation: exploring the party
sitting across the table from you.

NEGOTIATION IRL TOOL KIT

- Show them who you are. Be authentic and true to yourself.
- Lead with your unique value proposition (UVP). Do this by
  telling your story, defining what makes you distinctive, identifying your target audience, considering what you stand for,
  and executing a plan.
- Normalize. Set the parameters of what will be usual or standard in interactions with you.
- Know your superpowers. Leverage what you are good at to
  get what you want and reframe what you may have considered as a negative and use it as a positive tool.
- Share information thoughtfully. Ask yourself whether the
  information you want to provide is relevant, valuable, and
  significant to your UVP.

4.

Peek Inside Their Bag

How to Get the Information You Need to Negotiate from a Position of Strength

When I was a kid growing up in Washington, DC, in the late 1980s, I always wanted to know the daily weather forecast before setting off for school. Now back then, we didn't have smartphones that showed the current temperature, the day's anticipated highs and lows, and descriptions like "mostly sunny" on our home screens. You couldn't call out to the ether and say, "What's the weather in my zip code today?" and receive a detached response from Alexa or Siri. Nope, these technological advancements came much later in my Generation X life. So instead, as soon as I woke up, I would call a number that I remember to this day—(202) 936-1212—and listen to a prerecorded voice that told me what to expect.

Thunderstorms, rain, and excessive humidity were the three weather conditions that dampened my spirits the most. Booming thunder made me nervous. Rain meant outdoor recess and after-school sports were canceled. And humidity made my beloved press-and-curl hairstyle with tresses cascading down my back, known today as a silk press, shrink into the tiniest Afro you have ever seen in your life.

Now, we all know that no weather forecast is perfect, but armed with my phone-based prediction, I would prepare myself mentally, emotionally, and physically for the day. If I knew a thunderstorm was anticipated, I would have a mantra ready like, "That's just nature doing its thing. It's OK. You're OK." If the day called for rain, I would bring a book to school to read at recess or make alternate after-school plans. If it was supposed to be super humid, I would ask my mom to braid my hair to save me from its very public transformation. (Most of the other girls in my school had chemically treated hair, a "relaxer," and I was one of a few girls still rocking natural hair.) I would also bring an umbrella. I'd gathered the necessary information on the day's weather; I was ready.

Sounds simple, but at dismissal, not only were my fellow students caught out, but there was always a teacher or an administrator leaving the building holding their coat over their head. Umbrellaless, they'd try to run in a zigzag pattern, as if one could dart in between raindrops. I would always marvel that I was more prepared for the day than this person who was older, smarter, and more powerful than me. I had gathered information and then *acted* on that information . . . and that made all the difference.

Information is power. Information is the great equalizer. People often ask me how to negotiate when they don't have as much money, leverage, or influence as their counterpart. Of course, my first response is that you're a powerful negotiator when you show up as your authentic self and show them who you are. But my second response is that you must peek inside your counterpart's proverbial bag and gather information about who *they* are, because information empowers.

In any negotiation, information gathering is critical. As we discussed in chapter 2 on the Foundational Five, your first goal is to understand the positions (wants) and interests (needs) of the other person. Why do they want what they want? What is driving them? Where do their various needs lie in the hierarchy of needs pyramid? The information you gather may provide this kind of insight and knowledge. You also want to anticipate what the other person's alternatives are and how strong they are. To see what synergies you have, if any, and what tactics they are likely to deploy. You are finding out whether this is someone you can trust and/or easily come to a creative solution with, even if your initial wants and needs don't seem to match up. Perhaps you are also determining whether they are trying to take advantage of you, in which case every piece of information that you gather helps you level the playing field.

There are many ways to gather the information you need. I'm going to start with the most basic, and then describe some more advanced steps you can use if the negotiation remains at an impasse. The more information you are able to garner about the person you're negotiating with, the better your resolution will be. As they say, it's important to know thy friends—and often even more important to know thy enemies.

PEEK INSIDE THEIR BAG

How do you find out what you have in common with someone? The first step is to peek inside their bag. Not literally. I don't want

you to catch a charge. *Figuratively.* I use the bag metaphor because it reflects the fact that people are carrying around things
that you cannot see. Things that make them who they are. Things
that tell us what they want, need, or value.

Sometimes, the things in their bag are actual items. For example, someone might have tucked away in their briefcase or on
their desk a black-and-white photograph of their grandparents
who immigrated to the place they call home. That cherished
photo tells us that they are a person who values family and sacrifice; in a negotiation, that could translate into them being less
willing to take on a big risk unless they can tie the risk to a big
return on investment. Or a business owner might have a lami-
nated dollar bill in their wallet from their very first sale. That
carefully preserved memento tells us that their company and the
sale of its products mean a great deal to them, and that in an ac-
quisition of that company they may walk away if they are not able
to stay on as a consultant during a transition period to ensure its
continued success. Or a purse might hold a button stamped with
the words "I Have a Dream" or another slogan about freedom or
justice that gives us insight into its owner's ideals, values, and
philosophies. These are all things that you may also be carrying
in your bag. This is all information that may come in handy in a
negotiation.

Learning someone's perspective or what's in their bag without
making assumptions can be a challenge, but when you do, and
when you use that information to find common ground or build
a rapport, you increase the likelihood of getting the outcome that
you desire. The more you know about the other side, the more
material you have to work with in finding creative solutions to
your negotiation. Research can be time consuming, but time

spent early on often saves you time on the back end. Incomplete information about a counterpart often results in impasses and costly delays. Better to do the work up front.

Research

Information gathering applies to all three phases of a negotiation: the preparation phase before the scheduled negotiation begins, the bargaining phase during the negotiation, and the execution phase following the negotiation. The preparation phase may not seem like a heavy information-gathering phase, but it should be. Any negotiation starts long before you and your counterpart exchange your first words, whether face-to-face or via text, email, or a call. Once you learn whom you are negotiating with, the goal is to learn as much about that person as you can.

Just as in a job interview, you'll want to devote at least a minimal amount of time to doing your due diligence and researching the other party before your first encounter with them. If you don't, first, you'll look unprepared. Your counterpart might make judgments about you and your negotiation ability from this. Second, you may miss an opportunity to make a connection that may help you during the negotiation phase.

I always advise starting with online research. An individual's public social media accounts offer a gold mine of information.

What are you looking for? It's useful to know the outcomes of their previous negotiations, as that might offer clues to how they will approach this one. LinkedIn often lists professional successes, like promotions, deal announcements, and litigation wins. Personal or company websites often have a section for press releases that offer similar information on negotiation results. You may even be able to access articles that your counterpart has authored or coauthored, giving you a sense of how they think and their approach to bargaining or dealing with others.

Thanks to its 280-character post limit, Twitter, or X, can be a quick-and-easy guide to someone's personal interests. You might learn your counterpart loves white water rafting, traveling through South America, and coaching his son's youth soccer team. When you're searching for common ground, all this can be handy to know. Other social media platforms, like Instagram, Facebook, YouTube, or TikTok, can also offer a wealth of useful background information. One time, I saw two negotiators who intensely disliked each other form an unbreakable bond once they realized that there was someone that they hated more than each other: Alex Rodriguez, then third baseman for the New York Yankees.

If online googling makes you feel uncomfortable, which I understand, you should know that it is also common practice. I assure you that your counterpart is checking your social media accounts. Some colleges and universities look at these accounts during the admission process, and many companies screen social media presence when hiring. But this sort of online sleuthing is only one way to gather information on the other negotiator in the preparation phase.

Asking around your network is another way to research before the negotiation even begins. If you are dealing with a person involved in many negotiations, getting intel from friends and colleagues may give you a significant advantage. Miriam and Joel were opposing counsels in an employment lawsuit. Miriam gleaned from colleagues that Joel was a straight shooter but a bit stubborn and that he always anchored high with his first number, when his real number was usually somewhere around 33 percent less than his initial number. Before he accepted his bottom-line walk-away number, he would usually threaten to stop the negotiations completely. His signature move was to walk away from the table as a final pressure tactic.

Sure enough, for Miriam's first call with Joel, he was ten minutes late. Instead of apologizing for the delay, he spent the first five minutes talking about what ticked him off about opposing counsel on the prior call. During the conversation, every time that they discussed a contentious point, Joel would not back down. In fact, he became even more immovable. That was his way. When Miriam and Joel reached an impasse, Joel put pressure on Miriam to concede by threatening to walk away from the negotiation. Because of her initial research with her colleagues, Miriam was not surprised at Joel's tactics. She maintained her calm and was able to steer them both toward an acceptable number. If you've done your research, you will not be surprised either and can keep a negotiation moving forward.

Giving Info Helps You Get Connected

Once the negotiation has begun, you may meet your counterpart in person. This is another key opportunity to continue peeking inside their bag, especially if you have not been able to meet them earlier. Getting to know others can always feel a bit awkward. How many times have you been at a party and someone starts the conversation by asking you how you know the host, or where you went to school, or where you work? These are all basic, if unimaginative, ways that we try to connect. We ask these kinds of questions because we are looking for what we have in common. Here's a hot tip: you can actually skip right to the common ground portion of the conversation. How? By sharing something about yourself first. I am not talking about something deep and profound, like the reason you don't eat meat or why you go to temple every week. I mean something agnostic that is real. If you talk about your children, you're inviting someone else to tell you about their children, even if those children turn out to be their pets or nieces and nephews. If you talk about an amazing tattoo artist you know, you're inviting someone else to tell you about their amazing tattoos and who did them or that their religion doesn't permit body art. By giving information, we get information—and we connect.

Sharing something about yourself helps someone get to know you and opens the door for you to learn something about them. And yes, a social situation like a party might feel like a more natural place to do this than a negotiation. Often when people are engaged in an adversarial process, the last thing they are thinking about is how to share something about themselves. They're usually too angry or closed off. But sharing something about yourself works in this instance, too.

Ebony launched her virtual assistant (VA) company the summer after she completed her MBA, and she hit the ground running. She onboarded clients from various industries with enticing monthly packages that promised to solve their administrative needs. Ebony was so busy delivering on those promises that many years had passed before she realized that she had never increased anyone's rates, although the cost of doing business had skyrocketed for her. Ebony needed to pass through those costs to her clients. Ebony notified her clients via email about the rate increases. Everyone was on board except for one client, Joan.

Joan was one of Ebony's first clients. Ebony and Joan initially met because their children attended school together. The moms would always say hello to each other at pickup and drop-off. Then, one day, they started chatting at a parent association meeting. Ebony talked about her new VA business. Joan talked about her needs as a solopreneur, and the rest, as they say, is history. By sharing details of their new ventures, they gave information to get information, peeked inside each other's bag, and created the arrangement that up until very recently had worked beautifully for both of them.

Now Joan was pushing back quite aggressively on the new prices for the monthly packages. Joan wanted to negotiate the rates with Ebony. Ebony was surprised at Joan's reaction and, like many of us would, took Joan's attempt to renegotiate her rates quite personally.

Ebony thought that her 3 percent price increase was reasonable. Ebony also felt Joan's challenge to her rates was just another way of Joan saying that Ebony wasn't worth the price that she had quoted. Joan refused to pay the increase, and Ebony threatened to discontinue her services. Ebony, ready to just call it quits with Joan, contacted me for advice.

When Joan and Ebony's negotiations over price broke down, I asked Ebony if she had conveyed to Joan why her prices were increasing. Ebony said no. She had told her clients only that, effective immediately, the prices would increase. I suggested Ebony share with Joan how not changing her rates, which were well under market for her services, had hurt her company. Ebony told me that once she shared that information with Joan, Joan not only understood Ebony's reasoning for raising her rates but said that she, too, was in a similar boat. Joan shared that she was experiencing some hard times within her company and that though she was unable to pay the rate increase this quarter, she could start next quarter. Once they gave each other the additional information about themselves and their companies, they got the information they needed to understand where the other was coming from. Peeking inside each other's bag and giving information to get information had once again led Ebony and Joan to a negotiation success.

Role Reversal

When you know you are missing information and have difficulty figuring out the why of another person's want or need, you can use a technique called **role reversal** to put yourself in the other negotiator's shoes and ask yourself what you would do and why you would do it. You are essentially saying to yourself, *If it were me . . .* or *If I were in their shoes, I would . . .* For example, if you were a private seller of a five-year-old used car, you would sell the car as is with a buyer beware statement. You would not want to provide a warranty because you are likely no longer under the manufacturer's or dealer's warranty, and you do not want to be personally liable for a car you are no longer utilizing. On the other hand, if you were in the shoes of the buyer, you could understand why someone purchasing a vehicle would want additional assurances through a warranty or extended liability for the seller. When you use the role reversal technique, you are trying to reverse engineer why the other side is making the moves they are making, either verbally or in the agreement. Depending on how the person responds, you will receive either confirmation of your theory or new information to consider.

As we saw with Ebony and Joan, giving information to get information is often the most direct route to a role reversal. If you've asked the other person to explain themselves, you are often in a better position to understand where they are coming from. But asking them directly is not always an immediate possibility. Doing a role reversal exercise for yourself may help clue you in on the right questions to ask. Role reversal can also help you find a solution once you've confirmed your suspicions of the other person's why. In the car negotiation, for example, if you've determined why the private seller cannot give you a warranty (because they are no longer under the dealer's warranty), you might be able to negotiate with the car's seller, as an acceptable solution to your concerns, the opportunity to take the car to a private mechanic so that the mechanic can do a thorough inspection before final purchase.

Note, however, that role reversal cannot rest solely on assumptions. You have to make educated guesses consistent with what you actually know based on the industry, education, past experience, and—wait for it—your gut instincts. Just think about it: if you are buying a car on the last day of August, you might have a feeling that the salesman is more willing to do everything in his power to get the deal done so that he can count the sale to you in his closing numbers for the month. Or if you see a police car every ten feet on the highway, you might surmise that the cops are out trying to fill their quotas. If your family is the only family of color in your child's grade level, your child's teacher probably wants to be inclusive in their lesson plan, so telling your kid to do a report on Mahatma Gandhi, Sun Tzu, or Oprah was probably well intentioned. These are all good assumptions, but they also should be interrogated further. The point here is, to the extent you can, do the role reversal for yourself and then ask targeted questions that show that you do, or at least are trying to, understand where they are coming from. Again, their response will confirm or deny what you were thinking.

Travel Back in Time

Another way of peeking inside someone's bag is to employ a technique I call **travel back in time**. This technique is especially helpful when you and your counterpart are in conflict. Travel back in time tries to pinpoint some moment in time before the conflict began. It's sometimes less about gathering information per se, though it can be used for that, too, and more about reminding you who the person is and discovering what you still have in common. It helps ground you both in a good place, even if you are currently stuck in a bad place because of the conflict. For example, in a contentious divorce, I might ask the couple to tell me about their first date or their wedding—the assumption being that this technique would evoke a positive memory. Or if partners in a business are dissolving their company and having a hard time dividing assets, I might ask them to tell me about their first sale or the first day of their new business. By focusing on a happier time, you might find the momentum to get them through the present tough time—and learn more about where you are currently in the process. Remember, the end goal is always to be gathering information that can lead you to resolution.

Back in the day, I used to mediate community disputes as a volunteer mediator. This work took me all over, from schools to courthouses to courtyards of public housing complexes. One of the recurring issues was neighbor noise disputes. I'm sure you have heard this before (no pun intended). Downstairs neighbor believes upstairs neighbor is making too much noise. In response, downstairs neighbor takes their broom and bangs on the ceiling, creating more noise. It's a cycle in which people stop seeing people as people and instead see them as just human noisemakers.

In one such instance, the building management sent warring neighbors to me with the threat that one of them would have to relocate if they did not reach an agreement in mediation. You know what no one wants to do in the middle of a New York winter? Relocate. So the neighbors came in knowing that they had to reach an agreement, but that didn't mean they were going to get there willingly.

They hated each other. The upstairs family (Neighbor 1) included a young mother with a teenage son and a toddler daughter. The downstairs neighbor (Neighbor 2) was an elderly woman who lived alone. When they saw each other, they started yelling at each other almost immediately. I knew I had my work cut out for me. On the surface, they seemed to have nothing in common, but the one thing I knew that they had in common was that they had both made a decision to live in the building that they moved to. I wanted to help them to peek inside each other's bag, learn more about each other's wants and needs, and move them away from the conflict that had brought them to me.

I decided to try to get them to travel back in time so they would share information that might help them see each other as more than enemies. I started by asking them how long they had lived in the building and why they had moved into it.

Neighbor 1 told me she had moved in ten years ago when she was going through a breakup and her oldest was six years old. She wanted a good school for her kid, and the schools were better here than in previous neighborhoods. There was also more green space, which was better for a family.

Neighbor 2 said she'd lived in the building for forty years. She'd moved there after her husband died. Her son had been about six years old at the time, too.

Look at that. They had both revealed something that they had in common, but they were still too worked up to see it, so I pointed it out to them and continued.

"You said the schools were better here; what school did your son go to?"

Neighbor 1: "PS A1."

Neighbor 2: "My son went to PS A1, too. Was Ms. White still the principal when your son started? She was so mean."

Neighbor 1: "She was there when Anthony started. And she was still mean!"

They both laughed. You can probably picture the way the rest of the conversation went. They didn't walk out of the room as best friends, and they didn't even agree that the noise would completely come to a stop. But they exchanged numbers so that they could text each other if it got too noisy and they could communicate about it and resolve the noise disputes between themselves without getting the building management involved. Again, the information they learned about each other by traveling back in time and peeking inside each other's bag gave them just enough common ground to connect and continue their negotiation in a more informed and civil way.

Travel Forward in Time

As you may have surmised, you can also **travel forward in time** when you are stuck in conflict and don't see enough common ground to peek inside each other's bag. This technique asks you to think of a point in the future, a time that's after the current impasse or contentious dealings, a time when the negotiation has successfully concluded. So say a potential investor in a startup is negotiating with the company's founder. If they travel forward in time, the founder might see the investor's funds as key to the company's success, while the investor might see the negotiation with the founder ending in a huge payday. They might learn that they both share the vision that the founder's company presents a huge opportunity, like purchasing Apple stock when the company first went public in 1980. And that they are both excited about the end result of this negotiation, which will secure the generational wealth for their children that they'd never had for themselves. This common vision of their potential future success, and the excitement it generates, can get both sides of the negotiation to open up, find common ground, and offer more information to each other.

TRACK THE DISCREPANCIES

So far we've looked at cases where peeking inside another's bag leads to information sharing that points to a mutually satisfactory resolution. That is not always the case. Sometimes what we learn about others can point to a deeper gulf between our respective positions and interests, and we learn just how much we are *not* aligned. And sometimes the additional information may point to discrepancies between what your counterparts say and what they do. In that case, you'll have to keep peeking and eliciting information, but now you must begin to track these differences. The primary reason to track discrepancies is to figure out the source of the impasse. Is it due to a misunderstanding, varying linguistic styles, cultural difference, or something else?

Jasmine was invited to invest in a new business venture in an industry that was still in its infancy—the legal cultivation and sale of hemp used for its cannabidiol content (CBD) in the state of New York. CBD is not psychoactive like tetrahydrocannabinol (THC) is, and you can find it in teas, oils, lotions, creams, and other topical products. Various federal, state, and local agencies were, on a test basis, granting licenses to companies that wanted to be a part of the pilot program. Jasmine had a business contact, Dimitri, who asked her to participate in his fledgling company. Dimitri knew Jasmine from her success in the real estate market and made her many verbal promises and assurances in exchange for joining him as an equity partner in this burgeoning industry if she would invest $500,000.

As we've discussed above, I always encourage my clients to start with research. Jasmine had received an investor pitch deck from Dimitri, outlining some of his business plans. Specifically, Dimitri's deck focused on how the company intended to use the money Jasmine was being asked to invest. Jasmine had previously given Dimitri's company $100,000 and received in return a promissory note. Dimitri then came back to Jasmine, wanting more money for the machines that would produce the CBD. Jasmine was interested, but if she was going to give Dimitri more funds, she wanted to be an investor, not just a lender. Now she needed to do her research.

We examined the deck that Dimitri had given Jasmine on the new company. But beyond the specific use of Jasmine's money for the machines, there was very little information on the company's plans—or on this new industry. There was no mention of the volatility of the industry. Or of the fact that the business was not yet legal federally, or even in New York City. Or of their contingency plans for addressing this lack of legal status. None of the standard background information expected of a new company was in their deck.

It was also a one-sided term sheet. Usually, term sheets show obligations on both sides. This one talked about when Jasmine had to make her payments. But it didn't talk about when she would get the money back. It didn't talk about whether she had to be a shareholder for a certain period of time for her equity to vest. Or what would happen if she pulled out in six months. Further, it didn't spell out in any detail Dimitri's relationship with his other investors. And the agreements were devoid of some of the minority shareholder rights that you would expect to see, such as the right to vote on major decisions, the right to inspect the company's records, and the right to nominate and elect directors for the board of directors.

Jasmine's suspicions were growing. Many of the verbal promises Dimitri had made were not reflected in the agreements.

When Jasmine engaged me to negotiate for her, she was upset, annoyed, and ready to say, "No deal." She felt as if Dimitri wanted her money, not her, and that was a nonstarter for Jasmine. Jasmine wanted to be financially invested, but she also needed to be personally involved. She wanted to do everything from visiting the farm so that she could see the agriculture to discussing the manufacturing process for the CBD to understanding how they intended to market the CBD to the end users of the company's beauty and cosmetic products.

I asked Jasmine how well she knew Dimitri and whether there was a reason to not trust him or to believe that he was not negotiating in good faith. Jasmine told me that she had worked with Dimitri before on a real estate matter and that she didn't know why he would take such a narrow approach to her involvement in this transaction. She'd had good dealings with him in the past. Still there was some distrust at play; Jasmine was a Black woman, and Dimitri was a Serbian immigrant. Was Dimitri trying to take advantage of Jasmine?

We needed more information before she threw in the towel— and to track the discrepancies between the verbal promises Dimitri had made and the rather thin written material we'd received in the form of the term sheet and deck in order to be able to answer that question. Even the smallest detail can be enough to challenge our preconceived notions as to why a person is taking a certain position, approach, or stance in a negotiation. Tracking discrepancies helps you determine the accuracy of your own assumptions, get to know the motivations of others, try to find common ground, and take a deeper dive into the details of their business or their POV.

Jasmine assumed that she was being cut out of the more interesting aspects of the deal because of who she was. She wanted to be involved in the day-to-day of the company, but most important, she wanted her loan to be secured and she wanted more than a verbal promise to guarantee her investment. She needed to find out if her assumption that Dimitri might be trying to pull a fast one was true.

I advised Jasmine to ask Dimitri a series of questions that would help her understand what motivated him in the deal. She thought that, like her, he was interested in the novelty of the field in New York—and in the potential life-changing return on his investment. At the time in question, the legal, adult-use cannabis industry in New York was reported to be worth $3.1 billion per year.

When Jasmine and Dimitri traveled forward in time to the future, they found common ground. She wasn't wrong that he shared her excitement about the business's potential payoff. They both wanted the business to succeed and to generate a large return on investment. They both saw this investment as an opportunity to create generational wealth and start new legacies for their families. However, his interest and commitment went even further than that. Dimitri came from a family of farmers in Serbia, and he had always felt like the black sheep by going into real estate instead of farming. He saw this new business venture as a way to pay homage to his family and to continue their legacy.

Furthermore, when Jasmine continued her questioning and dove deeper into the discrepancies between what Dimitri had assured her of in their conversations and what had actually shown up in the documentation that she received, Dimitri let her in on a secret that I think is true about a lot of people. Guess what? He hadn't even read the documents! Dimitri had relied on his attorney to incorporate the deal terms that he had agreed to and then just forwarded the documents to Jasmine. Now, listen, I am an attorney, and I know that that could be a ruse that people use to point the finger at someone else. That being said, Jasmine believed Dimitri, and I did, too, because it is not unusual for businesspeople to hire lawyers to handle the legal terms while they focus on what they do best—the business.

To track the discrepancies, I had Jasmine highlight the commonalities and differences between her and Dimitri and how they understood the deal. I also thought this was best done, in this situation, one-on-one, businessperson to businessperson, without the lawyers involved, so that they could align their goals and interests. Eventually, even more details would emerge, as we'll see, that explained the discrepancies between Dimitri's verbal promises and the written materials in the deck. But first, given Jasmine's lingering doubts about Dimitri's full intentions, I suggested that she begin the negotiation with Dimitri by controlling the paper.

CONTROL THE PAPER

There is often a lot of debate in terms of who makes the first offer and who should draft the first version of an agreement between parties in a negotiation. If the discrepancies between each party's wants and needs are too large and you cannot come up with a creative solution to align needs, a stronger move may be warranted. In this case, you may want to **control the paper**. When you control the paper, you make the first move or first offer and you send the first draft of the agreement to the other side. The idea is that by making the first offer, you are playing offense and putting them in the defensive position. They are forced to respond to you. And their response may give you the additional information you need about who they are and exactly what they want. It's like peeking inside their bag on steroids. You are putting an offer out there to elicit additional information on the details of their position and even the why or needs behind that position.

When you control the paper, you are getting them to tell you how the specific facts that they are presenting make sense for this particular scenario. It lets you in on their bird's-eye view of the situation—and some of the on-the-ground details. You are also getting a sense of whether this is a trustworthy partner—or someone who is trying to manipulate you based on how they respond to your offer and how they mark up your agreement.

For example, if you control the paper and send your ex in your divorce a custody agreement that specifies you will spend an equal amount of time with your kids, and your ex returns the agreement marked so that he will have custody during the summer, he is sending a message with that edit. Controlling the paper has just given you new information to parse. The next move for you is, before just summarily rejecting his change, to find out why he's requested it. What is the reason behind his request for summer custody? Is he planning to take the summer off work so that he can travel with the children throughout Africa and give them a once-in-a-lifetime educational experience? Or is he planning to send them to sleepaway camp for eight weeks and totally shirk his responsibilities? Or something in the middle? What's really inside your counterpart's bag?

In Jasmine's case, she and Dimitri had already decided on the price of coming in as an investor. Still, our negotiating team took control of the paper. We drafted documentation that all sides weighed in on. Ultimately, the paper reflected their mutually agreed-upon understanding of the deal and its terms. This helped their negotiations and, ultimately, their relationship. Jasmine no longer felt like Dimitri was trying to take advantage of her.

By controlling the paper, we also solved the mystery of the discrepancies between what Dimitri had orally promised Jasmine in their initial conversations about the deal and what appeared (or didn't appear!) on the term sheet he'd included in the deck. As Jasmine reviewed Dimitri's revisions to the offer we'd presented, she pressed him to expound on why he was happy to expand some aspects of her involvement in the company while limiting others. Dimitri revealed that he had some majority stakeholders outside the US, and that in the agreements with those shareholders, he had limitations to what he could offer new investors in any jurisdiction. Jasmine, not one to just take anyone's word, asked Dimitri whether he could show her those external agreements. She told him that she'd sign a nondisclosure agreement and that if Dimitri's hands were indeed tied as he claimed, she would stop pushing him to expand her investor rights. He agreed.

The documentation Dimitri provided, albeit heavily redacted to protect his other investors' privacy, confirmed what he'd told Jasmine. There were indeed restrictions on what he could do. It wasn't ideal for Jasmine, but she was now able to resolve her final doubts. By tracking the discrepancies and controlling the paper, she now had the information she needed to place her trust—and her investment—in Dimitri.

Another lesson to this story: sometimes there is something external to your deal, such as other players, rules, regulations, or laws that you should be aware of. Again, always research and ask questions to gather as much information as you can, and consider bringing subject-matter experts onto your team.

WHEN SHARING INFORMATION ISN'T THE ANSWER

While gathering information is something I always encourage you to do both before and during the negotiation, there may be occasions when you don't want to give away your secrets. An experienced negotiator across the table may feel the same way. When I am negotiating, I am certainly not going to give my counterpart every piece of information that I have up front. I may want to time the reveal of my "real" ask for maximum advantage. And for many people, a negotiation is still seen as good old-fashioned haggling, and some people just enjoy the dance.

Take this classic example. You go to a farmers' market and ask how much a bag of organic peaches is. Farmer tells you ten dollars. You say, "I will give you five dollars." Farmer smiles and says, "I couldn't sell it for less than eight dollars." You counter with six dollars. You settle on seven dollars. Farmer goes back and tells her husband that you bought a bag of fruit for seven dollars that cost her $1.50 to produce. You go back and tell your wife you bought organic fruit for seven dollars that would have cost ten dollars in your local grocery store. Like I said, some people just like the dance of negotiation and the bragging rights that come with success. At the end of the day, you have to use your best judgment, regardless of what side of the table you sit on.

Here are some common reasons that you might want to hold back information.

You know that sharing the information is not necessary or relevant and, in some cases, may be illegal. For example, you are negotiating your salary and do not know the salary range of the new job, but you know how much you were paid for a similar position in a prior job. The recruiter asks you how much you were getting paid at that job, and you know that it is illegal for employers and their agents to ask potential employees in New York City (and many other jurisdictions) how much they earned in their prior position because of wage inequalities for women and people of color. Because you want your compensation to be based on your qualifications, you may refuse to answer this question and instead ask what the salary range for the position is and why.

You are the perceived underdog. Remember, information is power. Maybe you have less information than your counterpart, so you are less inclined to share what you know because you see it as weakening your power. I once had an arbitration in which the claimant was pro se (representing himself without a lawyer). He was very selective in the information that he shared because he thought sharing too much made the field even more uneven given that the respondent had legal counsel. Here you have to weigh the costs and benefits of disclosing certain details. He was right not to share because had he revealed that if he was not successful, he (and his company) would be defendants in several breach of contact cases in local court, then the respondent would have sensed his desperation, which would have informed their overall negotiation strategy.

You have a smoking gun. The smoking gun may be a recording, a text, witnesses, or other incontrovertible incriminating evidence that you want to reserve for later in the negotiation. Once I mediated a matter where the plaintiff shared midway into the negotiations recordings of the defendant saying the N-word. The plaintiff seemed to be waiting for what they believed was the right time to provide what they considered to be their strongest piece of evidence to support his allegations of discrimination and hostile work environment. He strategically used the timing of releasing this information to pressure the defendant to increase their settlement offer. It worked. You have to be aware that timing is everything when it comes to sharing your smoking gun.

You follow the principle of "give to get." Many old-school negotiators will tell you that you shouldn't give information without getting information first or in exchange. I once negotiated the sell side of a merger where the buyer would not tell us the identity of its investors until we provided a list of other companies within my client's portfolio that my client would consider divesting or selling to the buyer. You have to consider the value of what you are willing to exchange and whether it is of the same value or will be at some point. This principle is no different from what you used to do at the school cafeteria or when trading baseball or Pokémon cards. You want to make sure that at a minimum you are getting an equal exchange for your chips, mint condition Mariano Rivera, or an original Pikachu Illustrator promo card— or if you are lucky, more value in the exchange.

You don't trust the other side. Perhaps because of prior dealings with your counterpart or the information you gathered, you don't trust your counterpart and you are worried they will twist your words or attempt to use your words against you. For example, in many of the cases with police officers as defendants that you may have seen prosecuted on TV, the victim's family brings a civil case against the officers as individuals once the criminal case closes. A lot of the information, discovery, and testimony from the criminal case is repurposed for the civil case. The police officers are often very careful in their responses in the criminal case in order to protect themselves from self-incrimination in the civil case. For example, the privilege of asserting the Fifth Amendment of the US Constitution, among other things, is often treated differently in criminal and civil courts, in terms of whether the judge and jury can infer use of this privilege as an admission of guilt or wrongdoing. The Fifth Amendment protects against self-incrimination and double jeopardy and covers due process. Hopefully, your negotiations will not be this intense. Regardless, you have to determine what you feel comfortable sharing and consider the various ways the information will be used both in the present and the future.

Ultimately, in any negotiation, gathering information lets you know whom you are dealing with and what is really at stake. Sometimes, by peeking inside the other person's bag, you'll find common ground. You'll find that their wants and needs are more aligned with yours than you might have guessed. Sometimes you'll need to elicit even more information to find that common ground and confirm the basis of any discrepancies. And sometimes you'll need to control the paper (i.e., to expose even more about the other party, whether they willingly offer that information or not) to get a real resolution. Occasionally you—and the other party—may draw a line in the sand about sharing certain kinds of information at all. You do have to use your best judgment. Or get advice from a more experienced negotiator.

NEGOTIATION IRL TOOL KIT

- Peek inside their bag. Learn your counterpart's ideals, values, and philosophies.
- Research your counterpart up front.
- Give information to get information—and to connect.
- Use role reversal to put yourself in the other person's shoes and query where you are and how you got there and surmise where you might be going.

- Travel back or forward in time to ground yourself and your counterpart in a better place when there is conflict.

- Track the discrepancies to figure out the source of the misalignment or impasse.

- Control the paper. Go on the offensive by preparing the first draft of an agreement or making the first offer.

- Be selective about when you share information.

- Consider holding back information when the information is not necessary or relevant, you are the perceived underdog, you have a smoking gun, you follow the principle of "give to get" and you haven't gotten anything, and/or you don't trust the other side.

PART II

The Bias

5.

Be Heard in the Face of Implicit Bias

How to Negotiate through Prejudice

I'm frequently asked how I manage to get people on my side when they are coming from a radically different place. I talk to all kinds of people and get them to hear me, even when it seems that we are at an impasse. How do I create a rapport with people with whom I seem to have so little in common? How do I ensure that the other person feels acknowledged and simultaneously make myself heard, especially in cases where they may be making automatic assumptions about me because of who I am?

The usual answer is that if you want someone to hear you, you have to hear them—you must use empathy. As we've discussed in previous chapters, empathy and emotional intelligence are key to being a good negotiator, especially when it comes to peeking inside someone's bag. As is active listening. Yet there are circumstances where empathy can't solve an impasse. In those cases, you may be coming up against *implicit bias*.

An implicit bias is a negative attitude, often one we are not consciously aware of, toward one person or group. Our implicit biases prejudice us against one another and affect our behavior and judgment. Though we may not be conscious of an implicit bias, it still affects our attitudes in ways that may block, sometimes for excellent reasons, the very empathy we are told to use. When two people have little in common, deadlocks may occur because of others' implicit biases—or our own.

Intuitively, we know that most people don't want you to feel bad for them—they don't want your sympathy. People want you to feel their pain as if you were in their shoes. That's empathy. Yet there are occasions when you do not understand the other person's mindset or emotions, and they don't understand yours—and when they come into a situation with a negative attitude that they may or may not be conscious of. That's implicit bias.

Remember in chapter 1 when I asked you to identify the types of bias present in some real-life scenarios? Many of those examples were cases of implicit bias rather than overt, intentional bias. The boss who micromanages their employee twenty-plus years their junior may not think of themselves as ageist, but their inability to trust that a young person has the experience, maturity, and judgment to make good decisions autonomously may be revealing their implicit ageism. Similarly, you might protest that your decision to hang out and chat with a good-looking person despite your stated plans to head out from the bar wasn't rooted in a bias toward beauty, just a good time, but would you have stayed if the person weren't so attractive? That's lookism—and implicit bias. Or if you automatically approach a white male wearing scrubs in a hospital assuming he's the doctor rather than the Black woman sitting next to him who is also wearing scrubs? That's implicit bias.

When implicit bias is present, an unconscious assumption is often being made about you, the group you belong to, or the boxes you check. And that assumption can be flat-out wrong. To give it credence and "empathize" can further entrench these assumptions, rather than work to eradicate them. Implicit bias isn't always easy to identify, but studies have shown it to be widespread.

The Implicit Association Test (IAT) was developed by three scientists, Dr. Anthony Greenwald, Dr. Brian Nosek, and Dr. Mahzarin Banaji. The IAT has been taken by more than twenty million people, and according to the authors, their research was undertaken with the goal of forming "the basis of our scientific knowledge about bias and disparities." Among other findings, the authors' work showed that implicit bias showed up in 70 to 75 percent of Americans who took their Black-White implicit association test. The results revealed that implicit bias was more prevalent in white Americans and Asian Americans than in Black Americans. Simply put: implicit bias is measurable, it exists unequally across many spectrums, and it's probably affecting your negotiations (and your life) in ways seen and unseen, every day.

When simply peeking inside someone's bag and using empathy are not getting you the results you require, implicit bias may be at play. In this case, you need another tool in your toolbox. You must master the art of hearing others, and then *using* what you hear, to ensure that your position is received and understood.

HOW TO NEGOTIATE IN THE FACE OF BIAS

When people are in conflict and entrenched in their positions, they have tunnel vision. They see things only from their narrow perspective, and even if you are the most persuasive person in the world, you may not get them to see things your way—because your problems are not their problems. But what if you could *make* your problems their problems? Not literally, but figuratively, by replacing your cast of characters with theirs?

This is a key strategy for bridging a divide when two sides seem impossibly far apart: Make the problem that one side is having into something that the other side can relate to. Craft the issues in a way that appeals to the other party's sensibilities, mindset, and feelings. Get on the same path, to the same destination: one in which they are hearing you and you are hearing them. It's less difficult than you may think. As I've said, I do this all the time. And though you may need a bit of practice at first, if you follow the steps I show you, you too will be able to reach agreement with anyone who disagrees with you—even if that person is reacting to the situation with some kind of implicit bias.

What does it take to be heard in a situation where unconscious— or even conscious—bias is present? Here are the steps I recommend you take.

1. Downshift into a calm conversation.
2. Extend an invitation to the other person.
3. Gather information with a destination in mind.
4. Prompt them to reconsider their path.
5. Use final words to ensure arrival and be heard.

You can use the above steps even in blatant instances of implicit bias. And even when the bias is directed against your own family, as I, unfortunately, discovered. As long as you stay calm and focus on the process, you will be heard.

Recently, I had a chance to use these steps on an angry stranger, in a situation where I quickly understood that empathy alone wasn't going to help us find common ground. My family and I attended a holiday event in a communal party room in a friend's apartment building. My oldest son had to use the restroom (kids have to use the bathroom a lot, right?), so I walked downstairs with him to find it. We passed a gym on the way. Far away from the gym, in the lobby area leading to the restrooms, I noticed a cell phone on a ledge by the water fountain. I assumed the phone must belong to someone from the party, so I made a mental note to take the phone upstairs to try to reunite what I assumed was a lost item with its owner. It didn't occur to me that my ten-year-old son would also see the phone and have the same idea. I went in the ladies' room, and my son went into the men's room.

Shortly after I entered the stall, I heard an angry man's voice yelling at my son. I rushed out of the women's restroom, and the man turned his rage on me. He told me that my son was trying to steal his phone. I looked at him with dismay and surprise. First, because my son has his own phone and has no need to take someone else's. Second, because I soon realized this man wasn't seeing a child trying to do the right thing by returning a lost item, but rather an unfamiliar Black boy in his building whom he assumed was up to no good. And nothing I was going to say was going to change that snap judgment.

The man was screaming at Chase, and my attempts to intervene only seemed to make him angrier. I didn't understand why he or anyone would react this way over a phone. The man was quite worked up. He had convinced himself that my son was doing something wrong, and he was ready to fight. Never mind the fact that the man had intentionally left his phone on the ledge. I learned later that he had been working out in the gym and that the internet connection wasn't as strong there. He left his phone on the ledge outside the gym so that he could listen to a video that was playing on it. So when my son saw the phone, a video was playing across the screen. The movement on the phone was what caught my son's attention. He'd picked it up, waiting for me to return, and had been planning to bring it up to the party to search for its owner.

I tried empathy. Of course he'd been surprised at first to see someone picking up his phone, I said, but he must understand, now that he had all the facts, that he'd been mistaken. That didn't work. If anything, it seemed to make him madder. He was shouting, and my son was more confused than scared, though fear was coming fast, I could tell. I looked over at Chase, seeing the blank look on his face and tears starting to well up. *He's just ten years old*, I explained to the man. *He did nothing wrong. You can't talk to him this way. You're terrifying him.* This man, however, was unwilling to back down, and his anger was not dissipating.

Empathy wasn't working. I knew I had to try something else to have him see things from my point of view. If he didn't care about us, I needed to introduce some people or concepts into the conversation that he did care about.

Let me set the scene for you. We were standing face-to-face with my son off to the side but not in my peripheral vision. By this point in the conversation, I had asked the man to apologize to my son for the way that he was yelling at him and for accusing him of being a thief. He scoffed at my suggestion and looked at me incredulously as if I had requested a blood donation.

I took a deep breath, remembering that first it was important for me to **downshift** into a calm conversation.

I then began our exchange by **extending an invitation**. "Help me to understand where you are coming from," I said.

He paused and was quiet for a moment. I knew I had his attention.

Next, I began to **gather information**. At this point, my destination hadn't been completely formulated, but I knew I needed to be heard.

"Are you a father, sir?" I asked.

"Yes. I have two daughters, but I—" he said defensively, still in a hostile stance.

Now that I knew something about him, I would use the information he'd just given me to try to set us on a new course. And to prompt him to **reconsider his path**.

"How would you feel if an adult yelled at your daughters, especially when they were trying to do the right thing?" He blinked. He looked confused. He started to speak, but I continued. I was warmed up.

"Thank you. What would you do to protect your daughters if they found themselves in this situation?" I asked.

"I would do anything for my kids. However—" he started. I interrupted again.

"I understand. Do you have a wife? How would you feel if someone disrespected your wife? Do you have a mother? Sisters? Do you talk to them the way that you are talking to me? Would they be proud of how you are behaving, and for what? A phone? Help me to understand why you are so upset about a phone that we told you my son was not stealing."

I was on a roll.

The man was sputtering trying to respond to my questions. But note, his responses lacked the same fire that his prior statements had. It was like I'd lanced the angry boil of his outrage. I had introduced people who he cared about into the conversation, and he found it hard to maintain his anger, position, and posture toward my son and me. He was disarmed. But he still had not apologized to my son.

I had guided him to a new path based on the information I'd gleaned about him. But, of course, he still wasn't entirely hearing me.

My son . . . I was so busy focusing on this guy and getting him to do the right thing for my son and to hear me that I had not really absorbed what my son was experiencing. I looked over at him and saw he was paralyzed. When I locked eyes with my boy, he began to shake and cry. He just kept repeating, "I didn't do anything. I am not a thief. I do not steal." I could see that the entire interaction was distressing for him, so I put my arm around my son's shoulders and began to lead him away from the scene.

As I was leaving, I looked directly into the eyes of the man, and I said my final words. I had heard him. Now I needed not to empathize with him but to have him **hear me**. I said, "I hope you see that an apology to him is what would make this right."

I wanted him to apologize to my son. This was the ultimate destination. My son needed to know that the man's behavior and accusations were wrong. Now I had made sure that my want and need, at least, had been heard.

I left it at that. My son and I went up the steps, walked out the door, and made our way across the parking lot to our car.

Moments after my son put his seat belt on, however, this man appeared at our car. I was not sure what to expect. I was worried that he was still angry, and I wondered whether I would have to dust off the ancient jujitsu moves that I hadn't used since before my kids were born.

But I was also hopeful. I hoped that my last words had delivered that final "finish him" blow from the *Mortal Kombat* video game. Yes, I was nervous, but I was also optimistic that my words had worked their magic like a slow burn and that he had come to the car to say he was sorry.

And that is what he did. He apologized to my son. He told him that he, the man, was in the wrong. He thanked my son for wanting to turn his phone in. He told my son that he wasn't a thief and that he was going to have a bright future because he was thoughtful and kind. He then turned and apologized to me. He said that he had tried to return to the gym and work out after our conversation, but he couldn't. That after I walked away, he said, it was like I had planted all these seeds that had immediately started to grow, and they were crowding his thoughts to the point that he couldn't continue exercising. He had reconsidered his perspective on the situation. He'd been wrong. He had to find us to make it right.

He then answered all the questions that I had thrown at him. He said that he would have come to his daughters' aid the same way that I came to my son's side. He said he wouldn't have talked to his family members the way that he had talked to me. He said I was right in everything that I had said.

I accepted his apology because I know how hard apologies are to give, a subject we'll explore further in chapter 6. And as soon as he was out of my view, I burst into tears. What an emotional roller coaster. Our conversation had had so many twists and turns, ups and downs, and surprises—including the shock at the end that I'd accomplished my goals. *He recognized his behavior was wrong; he felt remorse and he communicated it to us.* He had reconsidered his actions and words. I had heard him; now he had heard me. I can work with that, and you can, too.

Downshifting into a calm conversation, learning to hear others by extending an invitation for them to share, gathering information with a destination in mind, prompting another to reconsider the path they are on, and then using final words to be heard and ensure arrival—all these steps to hear others and make yourself heard will work in situations where empathy and tactical empathy fail. You are still showing them who you are. You are still showing up authentically. The difference is that if they can't see who you are because of implicit bias or other reasons, then you put them in *your* shoes. You don't have to step into theirs.

THE FIVE STEPS OF GETTING SOMEONE TO LISTEN IN THE FACE OF BIAS

This is such an important topic—and these five steps are so powerful—that I want to dig into each one a bit further.

1. Downshift into a Calm Conversation

The first step in hearing others and being heard in the face of implicit—or explicit—biases is to slow things down like a Formula 1 (F1) car taking a turn on a tight corner. I love watching F1 races. F1 cars are designed to race at speeds of more than 200 miles per hour and take corners at about 60 or 70 mph. That means they are taking corners as fast as the average speed limit for highway driving in many parts of the US. To take a very tight turn, the drivers slow down and downshift. They then accelerate once they are out of the turn. This is exactly how I want you to see the timing of shifting into hearing others. When you are embroiled in a negotiation and things are heated or the pace is picking up, there are many things that you cannot control in that moment.

When I was arguing with the angry stranger, we were both engaged in a defensive spiral due to mirror neurons in our brains doing their job. Mirror neurons work like our brain's mirror. We unconsciously mimic what we see, hear, and feel. This happens with everything from imitating smiles to walking in sync to escalating anger.

The mimicking happens quickly. Yelling begets yelling. An insult begets an insult. A hit begets a hit. And so it continues. Some of the most life-changing events I've witnessed on TV happened in less than ten minutes. Philando Castile was killed in a traffic stop within forty seconds of being stopped. A veteran shot and killed his neighbors for shoveling snow onto his yard about one minute after the shoveling stopped. George Floyd was murdered in eight minutes and forty-six seconds. The point is that things escalate and can turn left very quickly.

Neuroscience tells us that when we are in conflict, we are unable to utilize executive functioning skills to make cool, calm decisions. Our prefrontal cortex, the part of our brain that regulates rational thought, is hijacked by our amygdala and we go into flight-or-fight mode. If you think about it, most people accelerate while negotiating, using the momentum to help them bargain or match their counterpart's zeal, anger, or rhythm. The best way to regain control is to slow things down and give your brain a chance to engage in solution seeking.

You have to slow down to shift the conversation, but you don't have to come to a complete halt. Just downshift, or manually shift the gears, into the tight corner in order to take it with ease.

How do we downshift when the angry spiral may have already started? First, you want to calm down whatever physiological response (heart pounding, sweating, yelling, shaking, etc.) your body is having at the moment. Usually, this can be done by focusing on your breathing for several seconds and trying to calm yourself down. I tell people to breathe through your nose for a four count and then exhale through your nose for four seconds. Nose breathing is inaudible, so it shouldn't be distracting to the other person, and it can really relax your body. I expound on other helpful breathing techniques in chapter 7. Second, you want to focus on what's happening in the moment. The problem that most people have when they are in conflict is that they are thinking about what happened sequentially prior. They are trying to remember all the points the person just made to address them. Well, to me, this is just as dangerous as looking backward while trying to drive the car forward. It can be very challenging to address everything that is happening and combat every point the other person made in the heat of the moment. I am trying to show you how to come out of a defensive position. I want you to control the things that you can, and controlling your body and next steps are within your purview.

It's helpful to focus on where you are going *next* in the conversation. Are your body language and tone aligned in supporting the conversational shift? Just as in racing or driving a stick shift, downshifting requires you to be aware of the conditions around you and make some quick mental calculations and risk analysis. Where is the best place to start the turn? What about the situation can you control?

Let's start with . . . your words. You can be intentional about what you say. Ultimately your goal is to turn the other person around as well and to get them to reconsider their path. That starts with an invitation to a conversation.

2. Extend an Invitation to the Other Person

It's often best to keep the invitation as neutral as possible. "Help me understand where you are coming from" is a phrase I often use. This lead-in to extending the invitation to others is key. Especially once you have been embroiled in a heated argument or debate. It's like throwing a piece of bread into a pond of ducks that are swimming in one direction. Once the bread hits the pond, the ducks redirect their attention to the food and will change course to get it. That's exactly why it works. The other person doesn't see it coming, and they are drawn to it because it is addressing something within them—you are feeding them. Asking someone to help you with something works because you go from being on two opposite sides of a conversation and in an adversarial posture to potentially being on the same side as collaborators.

Your voice when you make this approach will also reflect this collaborative intention. Your tone is key. You want to use a tone that expresses genuine curiosity and is not condescending or tinged with sarcasm. To be most effective, you don't want an upward or downward inflection of your voice. You want your voice to be the same the entire time, and you want to bring it down to about a five in terms of volume if you were previously at a seven or above before. In other words, you want to sound more like the announcer in a tennis or golf tournament—calm, quiet, and monotone—instead of like my favorite World Cup "GOOOOOOOL" announcer, Andrés Cantor, who is emotional, excited, and enthusiastic. Why? Remember those mirror neurons that I told you about? I want you to regulate your tone so that the other person unconsciously follows suit.

Keeping your tone in mind, you would say any of these lead-ins:

"Help me understand something."
"Help me understand where you are coming from."
"It is important that I get this."

If I am really feeling like I need to express more vulnerability, I might say:

"You lost me."
"I'm not following."
"I'm lost."

You would say the above statements, in the same voice you would use to say:

"Can you tell me if I need to make a left or right to go to the museum?"
"Do you know what the weather will be today?"

You want the words and tone to work together to calm (and, perhaps, disarm) the listener. Your voice should convey that you care about their answer and want to hear what the person has to say.

What is also key here is the thought process that they have to engage in to respond to your questions. On a macro level, you are interrupting the defensive spiral or escalating words and slowing things down enough to give them a chance to reengage their executive function and control over their emotions. On a micro level, you are giving them the runway to slow down on the track to make the turn.

Also, I want you to note that the lead-ins above are not questions, meaning that they are not formulated like questions grammatically and with question marks on the end. They are statements. Think of these lead-ins as your first bridge-building steps or even, more fittingly, the calm before the storm. The real questions come next.

3. Gather Information with a Destination in Mind

Before you can redirect the person entirely, you need more information about them. Knowing how to ask questions to elicit information is key in any negotiation, as we discovered in chapter 4. Here are three styles I often use: close-ended leading questions, a series of questions, and targeted questions.

Close-ended leading questions

Once you have the person on the hook with the lead-in statement "Help me understand," or the lead-in of your choice, you want to gather information that can, first, help get you both on the same page and, next, guide the other person to a predetermined destination. Where you want to go (i.e., the destination) might entail receiving an apology, assessing their hiring process, increasing your salary/benefits, or whatever you want the outcome of the conversation to be. In other words, the destination = your desired outcome.

When I teach my law students how to master this technique, I tell them to be the GPS (global positioning system) in the conversation. As the GPS, you set the coordinates and lay out the route by way of directions to a predetermined destination, which in this case is your desired outcome. The other person, however, is responsible for driving and following the path that you have laid out for them. In other words, in order for this to work, the person has to get there and feel as if they have gotten there on their own recognizance (and extra points if they reach the destination sooner than you had envisioned!).

Close-ended questions can be questions that have "yes" or "no" answers. Or they can just be very specific questions with a limited number of ways that the person can respond. "Are you a father, sir?" is a close-ended question. The answer is (usually!) either yes or no.

Series of questions

I like to ask close-ended leading questions as a series of questions, one at a time, with little or no interruption, by starting each subsequent question right before the person has a chance to contradict or rationalize their answer.

Recall my interaction with the angry man.

"Are you a father, sir?" I asked.

"Yes. I have two daughters, *but* I—"

"*Thank you.* What would you do to protect your daughters if they found themselves in this situation?" I asked.

"I would do anything for my kids. *However*—" he started. I interrupted again.

"*I understand.* Do you have a wife?"

As you ask this series of questions, you are gathering information and actively listening to hear and see how the person is answering your question.

First, listen for words that indicate a contradiction is coming. When someone answers the question and then says "but," "however," "nevertheless," or similar words, that often signals that they might negate or contradict what they said immediately before. To me, this denotes a potential shift in the conversation that could result in the other person taking control. If you hear a negative or contradictory term, gently interrupt to maintain control of the GPS and the conversation. I always make sure I'm interrupting with a polite phrase like "thank you" or "I understand" to soften the interruption and to help the person to feel heard.

Once he answered that he was a father and had two daughters, I had a basic piece of information that I could use to set the destination I had in mind. If he had said he was not a father, I would have still proceeded to other family-focused questions. He was seeing my son and me as outsiders to whom he had no allegiance. I wanted to figure out to whom he felt a connection and to introduce individuals to whom he would feel accountability.

"How would you feel if an adult yelled at your daughters,
    especially when they were trying to do the right thing?"
"What would you do to protect your daughters if they found
    themselves in this situation?"
"Do you have a wife? How would you feel if someone
    disrespected your wife? Do you have a mother? Sisters?
    Do you talk to them the way that you are talking to me?
    Would they be proud of how you are behaving and for
    what? A phone?"

Again, this is a series of questions with a specific destination in mind. You can also ask this series at once before the person has had a chance to get a single response in. Remember, you want to be in charge to control the flow of the questions and the pace. Asking a series of questions may make you think of cross-examining the star witness for the other side. It is like you are trying to learn about them, but you want to have questions that are designed to keep the person in their lane, so that they don't go off-road. You are trying to keep them in the hot seat while also learning about what matters to them.

How do you know what questions to ask? Your approach is often based on what you can see, discern, and pick up from their body language. I noticed that the angry man wore a wedding ring and that he had a unique accent. From the ring, I surmised that he may have had a family. From the accent, I surmised that he immigrated to New York from another country, and I was hopeful (prayerful, really) that someone had instilled in him strong family values.

I made the choice to target family-related questions. The negotiation that I was having with him was about my family, my son, and though he hadn't connected to me or my son so far, it didn't mean he would respond to questions about *his* family. When trying to figure out the best questions, trust your senses—what you can see, hear, and feel. You want the person to feel grounded and safe and not defensive. The questions should not feel like trick questions. They should be straightforward and simple.

The other thing about asking a series of questions is that at the beginning, when the person is hearing them, the person wants to respond. However, because of the one-at-a-time succession of the questions, and because ideally you are asking the questions with *little or no interruption*, they start to feel like hypothetical questions.

Perhaps the other person may be able to rally and answer your questions.

That's OK. The goal was still accomplished. You have made them reflect on what is happening. And you have gathered the information you need to proceed.

Targeted questions

Targeted questions are another way to gather information. They also help you figure out whether someone really is displaying unconscious bias. The goal of targeted questions is to draw the other person's attention to their own bias, if that's a factor—and help you be heard.

One of my clients, a company that actively promotes diversity, equity, and inclusion, had an issue recently that sent them into a tailspin. They had launched a grant program for women owned startup companies and notified the winners and nonwinners via email to inform them of their status. One nonwinning CEO, an

Asian American woman named Sarah, requested a phone call to discuss why she had not received a grant.

Sarah had made it very far in the interview process, to the final round, but did not receive a grant. The grant winners (with photos) were announced on the company's website. The winners were mostly comprised of white women, with a sprinkling of Black and Latina women. Sarah noticed, however, that none of the women appeared to be Asian. Sarah thought that there was bias in the selection process and specifically bias against Asians.

Whenever we don't get something that we want, it is natural to want to know why. Sarah was dissatisfied with the "Sorry to inform you . . ." email that the company had sent her. During the call, Sarah had some very pointed questions for my client.

"Are there any Asians on your board of directors?"

"How many Asians are employed by your company?"

"How many grant applicants were Asian?"

"Have you ever awarded a grant to an Asian-owned company?"

These questions sent my client into a panic. My client is as woke as they come, and they took it to heart that someone thought there was bias in any of their hiring, promotion, or grant-selection processes as it related to Asians. The client conducted an internal assessment and determined that they could do better in terms of making sure that their board, employees, projects, and grant recipients reflected their commitment to diversity, equity, and inclusion.

How did Sarah get the company to evaluate their processes and metrics? She asked targeted questions. Targeted questions are designed to determine whether there is bias. Instead of being accusatory and making a beeline to bias, you can use targeted questions to elicit the truth. Unlike with the close-ended questions, you want to ask these questions at a slower pace and in a conversational tone.

This approach works no matter what box you check. You can devise targeted questions to see whether someone is treating you differently because of your age, race, ethnicity, national origin, sexual orientation, and so on. Here are examples of targeted questions you can ask, depending on the type of bias you are trying to check for:

Age: How many women over forty are employed at your company?

National origin: From what countries do most of your workforce hail?

Sexual orientation: How many of your investors identify as LGBTQIA+?

Note that biases are not always based on the usual suspects like race and ethnicity and don't only show up in business settings. Bias could look like hiring people only from Ivy League universities, only dating women under the age of twenty-five, only having friends of a certain race, and so on.

And don't forget that there is often intersectionality in how we identify ourselves. If you check multiple boxes, devise your targeted questions to reflect your diversity.

All the question styles—close-ended leading questions, a series of questions, and targeted questions—can be used separately or together to gather information. Once you have gathered enough information, it's time to use the information to prompt the other person to reconsider the path they are on.

4. Prompt them to Reconsider Their Path

In my story about the angry stranger, I knew my destination. After taking a few minutes to recalibrate, I set my GPS coordinates to have the guy apologize. You can set the coordinates to any destination that you have predetermined. But how do you first get the other person to reconsider the path they're on, accept your GPS guidance, and thus ensure arrival?

One way you might begin is to take a piece of information they've given you and then ask an open-ended question that forces them to reconsider *their* position. For example, I asked the man whether he would want his daughters spoken to in the way he was speaking to my son. This was a strategic first step on my part. I wanted him to reconsider how he was speaking to my son. And to encourage him to take the road to the destination I'd predetermined for him: an apology. At the same time, I was giving him agency to make the move himself.

In order to get someone to step off their path and onto yours, you may need to ask a more open-ended question. One reliable opener is "Have you considered . . . ?" This construction is helpful because it is a noninflammatory lead-in. It doesn't put the other person on the defensive as long as your tone and what you say following this lead-in reflect this intent.

Here is an example.

"Have you considered how you would approach this if it were your [and here is where you fill in the blanks—son, spouse, home, job, property, deal, client, agreement, etc.]?"
    Or

"Have you considered what would happen if your family
learned of this incident?"

My next three questions would probably be: "What would
they think?" "Would they think you handled it the right way?"
"What would they think of you?"

Here are the similar lead-ins:

"What would you do if . . ."

"How would you feel if . . ."

"What do you think a [third person / neutral outsider] would
say if . . ."

"What do you think a third person you know would say if . . ."

Think of the last conflict that you were in. Ask yourself how
starting with "Have you considered . . . ?" or a similar lead-in
might have changed the dynamic—and the framework for what
followed.

The purpose of these more open-ended questions, as opposed
to the close-ended GPS questions we used to elicit information, is
to get the other person thinking in a direction that leads them
away from their implicit bias and closer to hearing you and
your POV. Further, an open-ended question such as "Have you
considered . . . ?" gives the other person more agency. You have
made them think about people they care about and how they
would want the person in their position to behave if a person(s)
they loved found themselves in this scenario. "Have you
considered . . . ?" invites them to reconsider their perspective—
and their implicit bias.

5. Use Last Words to Ensure Arrival and Be Heard

Using your questions to set the GPS and then prompting a reconsideration to step onto this new path is not just about getting the other person to see things from your POV; it is about making sure the thing you most want to be heard on is clear. You want them to arrive at your desired outcome. Your last words should be the last step to ensure that arrival.

First, you have already determined the end goal or destination. Was it to get an apology?

Was it to get an employer to revise the language in their job descriptions so that they are more inclusive?

Was it to get an organization to reconsider their process?

Was it to get a company to hold team members accountable?

Was it showing someone that you hear them so that you and your POV can be recognized and heard?

Your last words should be a final pointing in that direction. Whatever you want to stick and resonate with the other person. It doesn't have to be a loaded statement like what I said to the man earlier. Sometimes I say the following:

"It's your choice what happens next."
"Think about it and get back to me tomorrow."
"You should probably sleep on it before responding."
"If I were you, I would probably . . ."

In this stage of the conversation, you are using both your eyes and your ears to register whether arrival has been ensured. You want, you need, and you deserve to be heard.

Why does it matter when someone is biased against you? It

matters because it hurts. I'll say it again. You want to be seen and heard. You need to be seen and heard.

In my encounter with the man who thought my son had stolen his phone, I knew that my final words to ensure arrival and hear me had been effective based on his look when I said, "I hope you see that an apology to him is what would make this right." His defensive posture changed. His eyes showed genuine surprise. His epiphany wasn't immediate, but he had it. He arrived at our final terminus: where we'd confronted his implicit bias—and where we both felt seen and heard.

How to deal with implicit bias is discussed much more rarely than how to deal with overt bias. There's a reason for that. It's awkward to confront someone about behavior or attitudes that they don't even consciously know they possess. Denial or "I'm not biased" is often the first response when people are confronted with their implicit biases—and they (we!) may genuinely believe they (we!) aren't. Or they may get automatically angry or defensive as the man did in the situation described. But precisely because these biases are unconscious, we need to call them out. Because when others make assumptions about us based on our gender, our status, our race, and more, they are often introducing a negative attitude that needs to be addressed. When people are assuming we're the incompetent "kid" or the less-interesting "ugly one" or the lower-status "Black aide," we need to confront the prejudice. We need to make the implicit explicit. To help them reconsider their false assumptions. And to guide them to a destination where we are seen and heard. Because that is how we help each other—in ways that empathy cannot—genuinely hear each other and develop rapport.

NEGOTIATION IRL TOOL KIT

- Hear and be heard when confronting implicit bias. Focus on the process.
- Downshift into a calm conversation. Slow down. Give your brain a chance to engage in solution seeking by calming down whatever physiological response your body is having. Focus on what's happening in the moment.
- Extend an invitation to the other person. To engage the other person in collaborative solution seeking, use a lead-in such as "Help me understand where you are coming from" with genuine curiosity.
- Gather information with a destination in mind. Ask three styles of questions to elicit more information:
  - Close-ended leading questions. Formulate very specific questions with a limited number of ways that the person can respond.
  - Series of questions. Lead the person to a predestined outcome. Ask close-ended leading questions one at a time, with little or no interruption. Start each subsequent question before the person has a chance to contradict or rationalize their answer.
  - Targeted questions. Draw the other person's attention to their own bias (if present) and help yourself be heard by asking questions designed to reveal implicit biases.

- Prompt the other person to reconsider their path. Start a sentence with "Have you considered . . . ?" to help the other person reconsider their position.
- Use final words to ensure arrival to your predetermined destination and that you are heard. Make a final statement that will stick and resonate with the other person.

6.

Recovering from
Unintended Offense

When We Don't Mean What We Say

What do you do when you show up as your authentic self, get to know your counterpart, and then say the wrong thing—something that was received by the listener in a way that threatens to derail your negotiation? It has happened to all of us. We make progress developing a rapport or building a bridge and then we misspeak, use clumsy wording, or just plain put our foot in our mouth. They are offended, and we are befuddled.

Because we live in a culturally diverse society, we are not always operating from a common base of understanding. For a variety of reasons, both innocent and occasionally malicious, two people can interpret the same words completely differently. If you add implicit biases to the mix, you have a recipe for disaster. I see these kinds of misunderstandings give rise to conflict regularly in my work as a conflict coach, where I am asked to advise people on what to do *after* a disagreement has happened. Once an offense has occurred, we must find a way to build rapport again with the offended person, an unenviable and not always easy task.

That was the case when Carla, the owner of a travel agency, hired me to do a postmortem of what went wrong in a negotiation between her and Marco, a local guide/photographer in Panama. Carla initially had a good rapport with Marco, but after some further exchanges she realized that, at some point, the relationship had gone south. She had a vague idea she'd offended him but no idea what exactly she might have said or done to upset him or how to fix it. If she had slighted him, it had been unintentional.

To help her diagnose the situation, I focused not just on her actions but specifically on what words were exchanged between them. I always love these cases because it is like trying to solve a puzzle. I am really good at solving complex puzzles, and I am going to give you my secret.

My approach to this kind of "unintended conflict postmortem" has three steps. First, recognize that something you said impacted the conversation and created a gap between you and the other person. I call this "minding the gap." Second, identify what you said, in as much detail as possible. If your communication was written, dig out those emails. If it was spoken, look at your notes and try to reconstruct the conversation as best you can. Third, address the unintended offense directly so that you do not make the same mistake again. As we'll see, this direct address or apology is crucial to remedying the situation and getting a negotiation back on track, despite the oft-heard advice to never apologize and never explain.

MIND THE GAP: PINPOINT WHERE THINGS WENT WRONG

It was June 2020 when Carla first contacted me to help her understand what had happened during a tour she'd organized earlier in the year. Now, the timing of Carla's call to me is key to the story, because in the world at the time, two major things were happening. One, George Floyd's murder in the US sparked global protests and conversations leading to group and individual introspection about systemic racism, discrimination, and disparate treatment of Black people and people of color generally. For the first time, many white people asked themselves whether they were a part of the problem or the solution. Books like *White Fragility* and *How to Be an Antiracist* were flying off the shelves at Amazon. Two, the COVID-19 pandemic was slowly spreading across the world, and many people found themselves with extra time to ponder things while they were in quarantine or waiting for their industry to open its doors again.

As the head of a travel agency and as a white-passing Latina, Carla found herself with plenty of time to think as she waited for the travel bans to lift; like many others, she'd also begun examining her white privilege during the extended waiting period. She told me that the last tour group she led in Panama ended in disaster when Marco, the local guide, tried to renegotiate the prearranged prices and accused her of treating him differently because he was a Black Panamanian. She was completely caught off guard by his reaction. She wanted to know what went wrong.

My first step was to try to uncover when the gap between them was created. I asked Carla to "mind the gap," and recall for me the last conversation that occurred before she felt a shift in their dynamics. "Mind the gap" is a saying that is stated over the loud-speakers and written on train cars and platforms in train and subway stations globally. It calls each passenger's attention to the space between the train car and the platform and cautions you to pay attention so that you don't trip or step into the space. When-ever we feel a rift in a conversation open up, or we intuit a nega-tive reaction to something we've said, it's important to mind that gap in the conversation. The gap will always hold clues to the un-intended offense we are trying to diagnose.

Carla sat there thinking silently for a minute. Finally, she re-called the conversation when she suspected the gap had opened. It was the second day of a three-day tour of Bocas del Toro. She had met with Marco in the morning to discuss the plans for the day. At the time, Carla was updating her website and expanding her travel agency's package tours into other parts of Central America. That day felt like the perfect opportunity to get more than the usual touristy photographs of the travelers enjoying the iconic site. Instead, she hoped for some shots that captured the "essence" of Latin America for her new website. Carla tried to communicate her vision to Marco. It was in that conversation that things took a turn.

I asked Carla to try to identify what she said during the con-versation. "Marco, I want you to take more background shots to-day: shots that show the natural beauty of the island and the local fruit, flora, and fauna. I'd also like to get some B-roll of the mar-ket. I want you to record people laughing and having a good time."

Carla spent most of the thirty-minute pre-tour prep time talking about the photos rather than the tour route or the history of the tour. Carla didn't think twice about it: Marco was a tour guide and a photographer, and in her mind that day, she really needed his photographer side. Yet when Marco responded, she recalled, his tone had changed.

"OK," Marco said.

"Do you have any questions?" Carla asked.

"No," Marco said.

Marco's "OK" sounded different from the other "OKs" that he had said the day before, and Carla remembered thinking it was odd that he didn't have any questions. He usually asked great questions to customize the experience for the travelers. When I asked her about Marco's body language, she recalled that Marco had looked at her with an expression that she found hard to read. He seemed colder and more resigned, not warm and inviting as before. A gap had opened. It would take some further delving to figure out why, but we had found our starting point.

How do we know we've offended when it's absolutely not what we intend? How do we mind the gap? There are a few things we can do to monitor any unintended offenses we may commit. It starts with cultivating your awareness of the attitudes and opinions of the people you're talking to. In other words, it all starts with reading the room. There are three ways to read the room. One, you can look out for people's hot spots. Two, you can hear audible reactions. Three, you can feel the shift in the room.

Although some people have perfected their poker face, most people's reactions offer clues, even if very brief ones, to how they are feeling when they hear or see something they disagree with. Anthropologist Dr. Paul Ekman defines "hot spots" as the momentary conflict or gap between the words people speak and the sound of their voice, the gestures they make, and/or their facial expressions. Hot spots are always a sign of concealed emotion. Sometimes we are deliberately trying to hide what we are feeling.

Sometimes we are unaware of the gap between what we say and how we feel, and the hot spot is a sign of a repressed emotion. We may raise our voices intentionally—or unintentionally—even though our words express agreement. Our voices may quiver even as our speech expresses confidence. Either way, that brief gap or conflict between what we say and how we sound, how we gesture, or the face we make is a sign that something has rubbed us the wrong way or that something is emotionally off for us.

Of particular importance, according to Dr. Ekman, are our microexpressions, or the way we show our dissonant emotions on our faces, even if it is for a fraction of a second. A microexpression may be as subtle as a slight eyebrow raise or as apparent as a mouth agape. Microexpressions are universally understood facial expressions that display the emotions of happiness, surprise, anger, sadness, fear, disgust, and contempt. Our contempt may show in a quick raising of one side of the mouth. Our fear may show in eyebrows that are raised and drawn together. As a negotiator, you cannot ignore microexpressions because they provide valuable insight into what someone is thinking.

In general, it's always good to regularly glance over at both your counterpart and your partner—whether a spouse or a co-parent or a second negotiator on your team. Making eye contact as a reference point to check in can even save you from major faux pas. We have all been in a situation where you are saying something that you probably shouldn't, and on the other side of the room your friend, fearful that you are about to be totally canceled, is signaling to you with eyebrows raised and drawn together, an emphatic head shake, and the "jazz hands" movement to get you to change the subject. Pay attention to those signals.

Audible sounds can accompany microexpressions or stand

alone. People often sigh or exhale to express a variety of emotions, such as being annoyed, disinterested, agitated, and so on. A sharp inhale or catching of the breath can indicate surprise or being caught off guard. And, of course, tone is another indicator of how someone feels about something you have said. Carla distinctly remembered Marco sighing heavily when she told him she wanted him to focus on photography on the day in question. At the time, she hadn't really thought about it. But in retrospect, she realized that that was a clue she could have picked up on.

Another way to mind the gap is to pay attention to a shift in the atmosphere in the room. When something is said or done that is out of sync with the environment, you can feel it. It's palpable. There have even been some interesting studies on what a team of Dutch researchers at Utrecht University call the "emotional residue" of a place. Their studies show that emotions can impact one's physical environment both in the moment and even after the source of those emotions is no longer present in the environment. What we may casually describe as good or bad vibes apparently has a scientific basis in chemical signals, or chemosignals. The chemosignals found in sweat and tears may linger in a physical environment even after the humans who originally produced the sweat or tears have left. Thus the traces of the emotions that the sweaty or teary human experienced are still in the air. But wait, it gets weirder. In the Dutch study, researchers took sweat from individuals as they watched a movie that induced fear and disgust in the participants. Then, the fear and disgust samples, respectively, were exposed to different volunteers while performing a visual task. What's wild is that when the volunteers were exposed to the fear sample, they produced fearful facial expressions. Likewise, when the participants were exposed to the

disgust sample, they showed disgust on their face while performing the same tasks. The emotional "residue" the volunteers were
exposed to was catching.

These studies indicate that when you feel a shift of the energy
in the room, it's real—chemosignals or sweat residues may actually be affecting the vibes, good and bad. When Carla thought
back to when she and Marco had that uncomfortable conversation, the day his "OK" went from warm to cold, she recalled that
Marco was sweating. Marco might have been disgusted by Carla's
unintended offense. And what if the chemosignals in Marco's
sweat in turn induced disgust in Carla, causing her to show her
offense at his attempt to renegotiate? I am not a scientist, but it
sounds like the energy was contagious!

DIG FOR MORE INFORMATION: "WAS IT SOMETHING I SAID?"

Carla and I had, retrospectively, minded the gap and discovered
the moment the gulf between her and Marco began to open. Now
we needed to identify what had been said to cause offense. Identifying what you've said to cause offense, even when it may be too
late to change the situation, is important so that you do not repeat
your mistake. If Carla were still in the moment, she might have
asked a series of questions when Marco started responding coldly,
such as "What just happened?" or "Was it something I said?" or
"What's going on for you right now?" Since we were no longer in
the moment, we had to do a backward-looking analysis.

From the day Carla asked Marco to take the background
shots onward, there was noticeable tension between them. Marco
would still give the guided part of the tour with zeal and zest and

answer all the travelers' questions. However, his interactions with Carla were strained.

Everything came to a head on the third and final day when it was time to pay Marco. Although the terms of Marco's services were already set, Marco attempted to renegotiate his price with Carla. Carla pushed back, saying that Marco had not worked overtime and therefore was not entitled to additional pay. Marco's reasoning was that he deserved the extra pay for taking pictures, as she'd requested of him, on top of his tour guide duties. He then totally surprised Carla by saying that she was treating him disrespectfully because he was a Black Panamanian and she was a white American. Carla felt thrown off by the comment. She had shared with Marco the day before that although she had been born in America, her father was Nicaraguan and she was a proud Latina. Yet Marco insisted that she did not know what it was like to be a person of color growing up in Panama. He started to talk about the colorism that he experienced in his own country because he had darker skin. He already had to deal with being treated as a second-class citizen by his own countrymen, but he refused to be treated that way by her, an outsider. At a loss, Carla ended up paying Marco the higher price to make the conflict end, but as she sat reflecting on the experience during and in the wake of the racial reckoning following George Floyd, she wondered what she could have said or done differently.

In conflict coaching, when you ask someone to recount what happened, you usually get only one side of the story. As the conflict coach, you often must ask more questions to understand the broader perspective and fill in the blanks of what the other person, who is not present, might have been experiencing. Even if you do not have a conflict coach, this is something you can do for yourself. It was time to time travel back. I asked Carla to tell me about Marco and the first day that she had worked with him.

Marco grew up in Bocas del Toro and was proud to be a licensed tour guide. He had gone to school for tourism, and his license was something that he'd worked very hard to achieve. From what I gathered, Carla had made Marco feel devalued and disrespected by focusing her lens on his photography. She had inadvertently minimized Marco's main source of pride, being a guide, and that is why he asked Carla for more money even though he had not exceeded his committed time.

The moment we put the pieces of the conflict puzzle together, Carla knew we'd uncovered the source of the unintended offense. It just rang true. She felt badly that she hadn't been aware enough to mind the gap on the day the offense happened. But she did experience some relief at knowing what had occurred: she would never again make the mistake she'd made with Marco with another guide. Now she knew exactly what she'd said wrong.

Here are a few ways that you can identify your unintended offenses or misunderstandings promptly so that they don't create permanent rifts.

Lean In and Ask Questions

The first step after you've picked up on your counterpart's negative reactions is to never assume you know what the person is reacting to. Rather, you want to acknowledge the shift in tone, mood, body language, or words. Then lean in and ask questions.

The first questions are to yourself. *What happened? What did I say?* Maybe with a little introspection you might be able to figure out how what you said could have landed wrong.

Sometimes, it may not be so apparent. I recently taught a workshop at a university, and in my excitement about the course, I forgot to ask for everyone's pronouns during the introductions. I was following up on a comment that a student made, and I referred to the student's comment as what "she said." The class became quiet, and the student whom I had referenced looked uncomfortable. I first asked myself, *What happened?* I replayed in my mind what I said. I was not clear whether the class was reacting to my recollection of what the student had said or something else. Since I had not said much, I thought for a moment that it could be the pronouns. I was unsure, so I asked the class.

"What happened?" I asked. "I felt the energy in the room shift. Was it something I said?"

Another student raised her hand to tell me that Sam's preferred pronouns were *he/him/his*. It *was* something I said.

Checking in with yourself first is key because sometimes you can deduce what happened. See if you can pinpoint it first.

Next, check in with the other person or persons involved. Sometimes they will confirm your suspicions that it was something that you said or did moments before. Confirmation is great; it helps you move on and not keep replaying in your mind what happened or wondering impetuously what you could have done differently. Checking in with another and learning you're wrong is also valuable information. The other person may even reveal that they are reacting to something that you said or did an hour ago, a day ago, at your last meeting, or during your first encounter. Other times they will tell you something that you did not know.

Occasionally, the other person might tell you that the shift had absolutely nothing to do with you; you just happened to be there when they were reacting to something else. How many times has this happened to you? You sit there wondering what you did, then you learn in the moment that something happened before you got there between them and their co-counsel that affected their mood. Or that their stock was plummeting, and once they received a notification on their phone about it, that impacted the way they interacted with you. To add insult to injury, they might have been unaware of how they were behaving until you asked them about it. You just happened to be in the wrong place at the wrong time.

The two-part question, first the internal ask and then the external follow-up, works together like a checks and balances system. Think about it.

Adopt a Posture of Curiosity

If you believe you have offended someone with your words, and you have checked in with yourself and the other person, you should adopt a posture of curiosity. The goal here is to listen more than you talk. You want to be introspective.

On a trip to Ahmedabad, India, to serve as a guest lecturer at several universities, I totally put my foot in my mouth and managed to inadvertently offend my hosts. At the first university, I was invited to have lunch, and as we sat at the table preparing to eat, the director of the program asked me if I liked the food. My response? I smiled while saying, "I love Indian food." While no one pointed out my mistake, their microexpressions told me everything—I saw a flash of surprise and discomfort across many faces, and a few people exchanged looks with each other. Everyone became quiet for what felt like an eternity. Someone changed the subject, and we talked about the university until lunch was over.

I had no idea what I had done until later that day. I asked my guide if he knew what had happened.

He said, "Yes, Damali. You said, 'I love Indian food.'"

"I *do* love Indian food," I responded slowly, still not understanding the problem.

He said, "Yes. I know. But to us Indians, it's just food."

The lightbulb went off for me in that moment. I grew up in Washington, DC, and had lived in Georgia, California, and New York. I had been exposed to every type of cuisine imaginable. In DC, it was common to say, "Let's go out for Chinese food" or "Are you in the mood for Ethiopian food tonight?" I approached that conversation in the conference room in Ahmedabad from an American perspective, given that America is such a melting pot of cuisines. Yet by referring to the food as "Indian food," I committed a major faux pas. Somehow, I implied that the food that one billion people eat and that differs widely across the country was a certain type of food. It was unintentionally offensive.

If I had not adopted a posture of curiosity and checked in with my guide, I would have never figured out that I had offended my hosts while trying to give them a compliment about the food. That was a pretty innocuous example of saying something that I did not mean in the way that it landed. It was a onetime occurrence.

A NOTE ON ADOPTING A POSTURE OF CURIOSITY AND ALLYSHIP

People ask me all the time how to show that they are allies. Let me start by telling you what not to do. Do not say things like "I have a Black friend," "My wife is Asian," "We adopted a Latino baby," or "My son's best friend is gay." I understand why you are doing it. You are trying to connect with the person across from you and show them that you have something in common. It is an admirable approach to try to find common ground. Often, however, it falls flat because knowing or being related to someone who checks the box is not the same as checking the box yourself. It can come across as claiming a false sense of understanding.

Adopting a posture of curiosity is a much better route to allyship. Adopting a posture of curiosity means being open to hearing something uncomfortable. It means learning something about the other person and about yourself in the process. It means replacing the defensive mechanism that often results in statements of "allyship" with an open mind and an open-ended question.

Examples of things you can say:

Tell me more.
What else?
Give me more context.

REPAIR THE DAMAGE: THE POWER OF A CLEAR STATEMENT

Once you have minded the gap and identified your unintended offense, you'll want to address the gap and fix it with a clear statement. In Carla's case, if she'd identified the gap on the spot, she could have told Marco outright that what she should have said was that she very much valued his tour guide services and the time he put into them, and asked whether he was OK with adding his photography services as well.

Starting with a statement that clearly addresses the miscommunication is always a constructive way to proceed. Some options for what you can say are:

"What I should have said was . . ."

"You know earlier I said X—that's not what I meant. What I meant to say was Y."

"That's not what I meant. Do you know what I am trying to say?"

"I think there was a disconnect between what I had intended and how it landed."

If appropriate, consider inserting some humor. Sometimes humor can defuse tension.

"Now I sound like [insert the name of a public figure known for saying something similar]."

"I am known to put my foot in my mouth."

"I always mix up sayings."

Acknowledging the unintended offense and clarifying what you meant to say will go a long way to reestablishing rapport with the offended person. For some people, just letting them know that you recognized the offense is enough. For others, a little more discussion may be required to bridge the gap between intent and impact.

Address the Impact, Not the Intent

Often a disconnect exists between intent and impact in communication. Intent is what you meant or had in mind when you spoke, and impact is how it was received by the other person. You have no control over how the person will receive the information. Intentions are great, and of course, we all prefer good intentions to bad intentions, but when it comes to negotiations and unintended offenses, the best way to get things back on track is to focus on the impact of what you said and not your intentions.

Think about it like this. Someone might hit your car while trying to rush their wife to the hospital to give birth, or they might hit your car while texting a friend about a party. The baby story sounds better, but the damage to your car, and thus the impact on you, is the same. You can't drive your car for a week while it is in the shop being repaired. When I was a kid, I was hit by a car that made a turn at a red light where there was a sign that said, "No right turn on red." Turned out he was a basketball player who was running late to a game, so he made the illegal turn. His intentions didn't matter. The harm was done, and I spent a few days in the hospital and several days out of school.

When your words or actions have had a negative impact on

others, you have to fix the relationship, whether or not you intended the harm. Real-life negotiations involve people who have feelings, thoughts, and egos. As we saw with Marco, Carla's intention mattered less than the impact of her request that Marco give up his guide responsibilities to photograph scenery. To successfully get what you want, you have to remove the impediments that arrive during the course of the negotiation. Don't get stuck on whether you intended to offend someone. Address the impact.

Apologies Repair Relationships

I've been taught time and time again, in almost every negotiation course that I've ever taken, to not apologize in a negotiation. They told me that apologies bring attention to mistakes. I have always found this logic to be flawed and to be the wrong message to teach negotiators. You shouldn't be afraid to apologize for a misstep or saying the wrong thing. It's also fine to acknowledge that facts or situations have changed and that the new information you're sharing may contradict something that was said or done previously. Negotiations should be a forgiving, self-correcting process.

Trust is required for smooth and mutually beneficial interactions and social relationships. Yet trust is fragile and can easily be broken, even by innocuous mistakes and misunderstandings. The good news is that apologies work. Study after study shows that trust can be reestablished in a relationship or a negotiation if the person who committed the offense apologizes. This repair function of apologizing cannot be underestimated. Rather than equating apologies to personal blame, if we focused on apologies and moving toward rebuilding personal credibility, we would live in a healthier society with healthier relationships—and healthier negotiations. It's probably no accident that a study showed that existing interpersonal relationships can be improved by increased forgiveness and that women tend to be more forgiving than men—women also tend to have stronger, more trusting relationships.

Note that I am not suggesting that one person should hastily trust another in a negotiation. Definitely do not do that. Plus, in a negotiation if people get something wrong, I want them to fix it. When I get something wrong, I try to fix it. I have said countless times, "I realize that's not what I intended to say; I wanted to say this instead." On each occasion, I acknowledged my unintended offense and built more trust with that person. I know this is hard for a lot of us. It may be especially hard for BIPOC, whom studies show tend to feel more pressure not to make a mistake because we are often judged more harshly than our peers who commit the same error. But admitting that what you said may have hurt someone may fix the relationship. And ultimately that may matter more than the temporary discomfort of acknowledging your mistake, intentional or not.

If you are wrong and realize it, avoid the urge to be silent and hope that the issue will go away. In the moment, or perhaps later when you have had a chance to reflect, apologize and explain why you think an apology is warranted. Say, "I am sorry when I said or did X because . . ." Make sure the apology is genuine. What happens when you give an apology? An apology changes the atmosphere, costs nothing, and demonstrates humility and caring. If sincere, an apology can make all the difference in building, or rebuilding, trust and respect. The power of a sincere apology is unmatched.

A few years ago, I served as a conflict coach for a nonprofit organization that had a program intended to interrupt the school-to-prison pipeline by giving individuals accused of misdemeanors the option to go to a set number of conflict coaching sessions in lieu of juvenile detention. Because I was new to conflict coaching at the time, I was paired with an older white man who was a seasoned conflict coach. Let's call him Paul. I had met Paul before because we were both mediators, but he and I had never handled a case together.

We briefly discussed how to approach the coaching session, and then the client—let's call him Jamal—walked into the room. Jamal sat in the seat across from Paul. I sat at the head of the table so that Jamal was to my left and Paul was to my right. The session started off easily with introductions and pleasantries. Paul then started the conflict coaching process and proceeded to summarize what he had heard Jamal say. Paul began to share what Jamal's options were given the conflict. Jamal started shaking his head as if he did not agree with what Paul was saying. To which Paul said in response, "Jamal, stop resisting."

Jamal froze. I caught my breath. Paul continued to talk. He seemed unaware of the impact of the words "Stop resisting," even though there had been a palpable shift in the energy in the room.

If you are reading this and don't understand why those two words would make a young Black man freeze and make me catch my breath, then let me explain. "Stop resisting" is a phrase often used by US law enforcement to justify unreasonable use of force while detaining a Black or Brown person. In short, "Stop resisting" can be very triggering for Black people, and it was clear from Jamal's body language and his microexpression—his body became very still, and his upper eyelids were raised super high—that he was triggered. I even found myself being triggered, and I was raised by a cop and had spent several years training New York City cops in mediation and conflict de-escalation. But of course, this wasn't about me. It was about Jamal. And because of Paul's choice of words, which had an unintended impact on Jamal, Jamal was about to lose an opportunity for a clean slate.

Back in the conference room, Paul probably said "Stop resisting" four more times within the next hour. Upon Paul's last utterance of the phrase, Jamal raised his hands in the air as if he were giving up and said, "I'm not resisting!" Jamal looked at me, and his eyes very clearly conveyed a silent plea to make the situation stop. I called for a ten-minute break with the goal in mind of helping Paul understand the impact of his words on Jamal and on the conflict coaching process. Plus, Paul, whom I knew to be a nice and well-intentioned guy, was giving Jamal the wrong impression of himself.

During the break, I explained to Paul as amicably as I could the impact of "Stop resisting" when said by a white male to a Black or Brown person, especially a Black male who was in court-mandated conflict coaching after a run-in with the law. Paul was dumbfounded and raised his eyebrows. It was several seconds before he said anything.

I asked him if it was OK for me to recount the last hour from my perspective to show him when the conversation had shifted. I walked Paul through the three-step conflict postmortem. I showed him how the gap was created when he said "Stop resisting" the first time. And how every subsequent time Paul said that phrase, Jamal froze and raised his upper eyelids. I pointed out that at the end Jamal even raised his hands in the air and said loudly, "I'm not resisting." Together we clearly diagnosed the misunderstanding and offense involved in using those words with someone like Jamal. It was at step three, addressing the unintended offense by fixing it with a clear statement, that Paul asked for my help. We had about forty minutes remaining in our conflict coaching session with Jamal. Paul wanted to find a way to build a bridge again with Jamal, so that Jamal could benefit from the program.

To execute this final step, I suggested that Paul use a combination of two techniques: (1) an apology and (2) fixing it with a clear statement. Although unintentionally, Paul had alienated and offended Jamal, and Jamal was now less receptive to the whole process. To me, any chance of moving forward and saving the relationship and rapport required an admission of fault first.

Then, fixing it with a clear statement.

We started part two of the session.

Paul said, "Jamal, during the break Damali brought something to my attention, and I owe you an apology."

Jamal froze, but this time in a more relaxed posture.

Paul continued, "I apologize for using the phrase 'Stop resisting' and for using it so many times in the prior session. I should not have used that phrase because, after speaking with Damali, I now understand how it sounds when I say it to you, and I did not mean to have that impact on you. What I should have said was 'Keep an open mind' because that is really what I meant. I think Damali and I have some good options for you to consider. If we can start over in the time we have left, I will try to be more cognizant of my word choice going forward. What do you think?"

I was so proud of Paul. The coaching session was back on

track, and Jamal was not only receptive to our ideas to keep him out of the prison system but also added some ideas of his own. If Paul had started the second session by trying to rationalize his intentions when he said "Stop resisting," he would have completely lost Jamal's trust and Jamal might have forgone the opportunity to make some changes in his life. The apology and clear statement did not just fix the misunderstanding, it also gave Jamal the opportunity to solve his problems.

Paul's final question was also a good way to conclude his apology. By ending with a "What do you think?" to the offended person, you restore their sense of agency. I always like to pose an open-ended question to the person who was offended at the end of the apology or clear statement. Why? Because it puts them back in the driver's seat to decide what happens next.

No one is perfect, and we have all unintentionally offended someone—maybe you even did it today. Figuring out what happened is not only the right thing to do but is also restorative. Paul's willingness to acknowledge fault and offer a clear statement of the misunderstanding was a good resolution for Jamal, but it was also a good resolution for Paul. Paul learned how to recover when he unintentionally offended someone with his words. Jamal learned that people don't always say what they mean, and people don't always mean what they say.

I want you to be proactive in trying to address a situation when you become aware that something you said or did offended someone else. This may feel uncomfortable at first because it is common to become defensive. As a first response to the other person, resist the urge to try to rationalize what you said or invalidate the other person's feelings when they are explaining how you unintentionally made them feel. Rather, make a clear statement, such as "I realize that's not what I intended to say; I wanted to say this instead," or a clear apology, such as "I am sorry for when I said or did X because . . ." I promise you the repair in the relationship will be well worth it.

NEGOTIATION IRL TOOL KIT

- When offense has occurred, do not ignore it. Build rapport again with the offended person. If you aren't sure what the offense was, do an unintended offense postmortem.
- Mind the gap. Recognize that something you said impacted the conversation and created a gap between you and the other person.
- Look out for people's hot spots. Listen for audible reactions. Detect a shift in the room.
- Dig for more information. Lean in and ask questions while adopting a posture of curiosity.
- Repair the damage. Address the unintended offense directly so that you do not make the same mistake again.
- Focus more on the impact than the intent. Fix the relationship when your words or actions have had a negative impact on others, whether or not you intended the harm.
- Fix it with an apology and a clear statement. Remember, negotiations should be a forgiving, self-correcting process.

7.

Negotiating
When You're the Target

"The Talk" and Other High-Stakes Negotiations

I sat on the edge of my bed, clutching my white terry cloth robe around me, still in shock. Moments before, I'd been sleeping soundly next to my boyfriend in my studio apartment in Washington, DC. Five minutes later, my life had changed.

It had been just shy of 6:00 a.m. when I was jolted awake by pounding at my door, followed by a booming voice.

"FBI. Is Kevin in there?"

What? FBI? I must be dreaming. I'd fallen asleep to the hit show *24*, just as Kiefer Sutherland, playing the role of Jack Bauer, ended a firefight between the Federal Bureau of Investigation (FBI) and a terrorist group. Now an unfamiliar voice was at my door telling me they were FBI—and to open up. Had the show come to me? I really must be dreaming.

I looked out the front window. My street, which was one way going from east to west, was completely blocked off. Police cars and nondescript government cars for as far as I could see lined the narrow street.

"Did you say FBI?" I inquired. My heart dropped. Were they going to come in shooting first and asking questions later? Why was the FBI at my house? My vision blurred. Twenty questions popped into my head at once. My heart was racing.

He continued. "Yes, ma'am. And Department of Homeland Security [DHS] and the DC and Maryland police," the voice responded. "Is Kevin in there?"

What in the entire f——? Did he just say that four agencies were at the door of my three-hundred-square-foot apartment? The dream was now a nightmare.

I looked out the side window. Armed agents and officers were standing with guns drawn in the narrow passageway that separated my house from my neighbor's house.

Who did they think was in my house? Pablo Escobar? Clearly, the intel was wrong; it was just my boyfriend and me. Kevin . . .

Wait . . . they said his name. When they said "FBI" the first time, they said his full name.

Kevin responded calmly, "I am here."

Stay alive. Stay alive. Stay alive.

I breathed in and out to try to slow down my heart rate to a steady pace. I needed to think clearly. I didn't know what was going on or why four agencies were looking for him. What I did know was I was outmanned, outgunned, and out of options. The only thing that I could do was open the door.

But I was terrified. Every hair on my body was standing at attention. The threat level to me was at a 10 out of 10. I had seen *24*, but I also knew that in real life, things didn't always work out for people who looked like me. That sometimes just being born with Black or Brown skin was perceived as a threat.

I knew that I could easily become a target or collateral damage. I was not afraid of law enforcement per se. I was raised by a United States Marine Corps vet and a thirty-year veteran of the Metropolitan Police Department (MPD), the police force of Washington, DC. I was probably the most prepared person to be in a standoff with the police and their friends the FBI and DHS's US Immigration and Customs Enforcement (ICE) division.

I looked at my boyfriend again. *They are here for Kevin*, I thought. *I am not the target. I am not the target. I am not the target.* I repeated in my head three times. I then took about sixty seconds to think about what I was about to say and do next.

"I am going to open the door," I said. "We are the only two people here in a studio apartment. We are unarmed." I heard a stir. *Did they believe me? Isn't that what someone would say if they were actually armed? I hope not.* I opened the door. I didn't get shot. Point Damali.

It was just like a scene from *24*. Nothing less than a full infantry was lining the staircase leading up to my floor and flanking the walls of the hall in front of my apartment. Everyone was armed. I didn't see any women. No smiles. They were wearing bulletproof vests. I was in pajamas and a robe, but I felt like I was naked.

Several men entered at once, and they filled my apartment—it was quite small. One took a manila folder out from under his bulletproof vest. His other hand remained just slightly above his gun. Physically, I was paralyzed, but my brain kept churning.

Don't get shot, I thought.

I have been pulled over for speeding, expired tags, and a broken taillight. I have been frisked visiting prisons in the US and Europe. I have been in many scary situations (some of my own doing and inherently more dangerous, like climbing the active volcano Concepción on the Isla de Ometepe in Nicaragua without ropes or hiking boots). However, I have never experienced anything like a four-agency pursuit in my entire life, and I never want to experience it again. It was a seemingly impossible situation. And though nothing can ever completely prepare us for this kind of incident, one of the reasons I wrote this book in the first place—and why I do the work I do every day—is to help you negotiate the impossible.

Remember, first and foremost, negotiation is an art and not a science. No two negotiations are the same. Throughout this book I have provided you with different strategies designed to accomplish your goals and to result in a successful negotiation. This chapter is no different—except that this time, your ultimate goal is to survive, and a successful outcome in this instance is living to negotiate another day.

When I was eleven years old, I wrote a poem that I delivered as a rap in a local summer youth competition where kids throughout Washington, DC, competed for small monetary prizes. I wore a baby-pink Champion short set, bright white slouch socks, and high-top Reeboks. I looked like MC Lyte, I sounded like Queen Latifah, and I won for my category. The poem was "Don't End Up Being Another Dead Black Man." The chorus was catchy, and by the time I got to the third refrain, the crowd was singing it with me. "Live your life. Do the best you can. Don't end up being another dead Black man."

Decades later, when the FBI and their buddies came to my

home, I heard this refrain playing in my head like a mantra. And even though the lawyer in me wants to explain qualified immunity (the doctrine that generally shields the police from civil liability), and the professor in me wants to engage you in a policy reform discussion, it's the Black mother in me who thinks it's time that we have "The Talk."

TALKING ABOUT "THE TALK"

Many Black people already understand this. Something many people of color, especially Black men and women, have in common is "The Talk"—a conversation about what to do (and what not to do) when you are stopped by the police. Most Black people I know have either received The Talk or had to give it to their own kids. The Talk has morphed over generations and across geographic locations. I recall my maternal grandparents, who were a part of the Great Migration—they hailed from South Carolina and put down roots in Washington, DC—telling me about growing up in the rural South, where lynching, Jim Crow laws, and segregation were the norm. They have since passed away, but I am willing to bet that The Talk they gave to my mother and her five siblings was slightly different than The Talk my siblings and I received. Why? Well, first, just as with any oral history, the versions will change like a game of telephone. Second, The Talk has to evolve as the world changes.

Three major changes since my grandparents' days? Smartphones, social media, and bodycams. Victims and bystanders alike take out their smartphones to record what's happening and share the stories. Social media transmits those stories, and in a short period of time an incident in Minnesota goes viral. Plus, many police officers have bodycams, the footage of which police departments can release to the public. Despite these advancements in technology that give us more transparency and should lead to greater accountability and the reduction of these incidents, the need for The Talk remains.

The Talk is given in the Black community from elders and parents to children, young kids, and teenagers. In part, it's a cautionary message that they may be judged not on the content of their character as Reverend Dr. Martin Luther King Jr. stated in his famous "I Have a Dream" speech. Rather, it reveals the harsh reality that they will be judged on the color of their skin. In part, it's an empowerment tool that gives our sons and daughters a playbook of what to do, at the end of the day, to survive. Dr. Broderick Leaks, licensed clinical psychologist and vice chair for student mental health in the Department of Psychiatry and Behavioral Sciences at the University of Southern California, calls The Talk "prepping your children for the realities of society that they have to navigate."

Before I give you the version of The Talk that I give my own two sons, it is important to me that you know more about me and where I am coming from. I am a Black American woman raised by a Black policeman. I have five Black brothers, two Black sons, and one Black husband. I have also personally trained hundreds of New York police officers on how to de-escalate conflict with their words instead of their weapons. I also have an uncle who was brutally beaten by the police in the Midwest in the 1970s when he was in his twenties. On the evening of January 6, 2021, the day that domestic terrorists breached the US Capitol in Washington, DC, my hometown, one of my brothers was stopped by the Army National Guard. While holding an assault rifle, the soldier asked my brother (who was riding a bike home from work) why he was outside after curfew. My brother was shocked. Curfew? On the day of the breach, the DC mayor had instituted a citywide curfew that went into effect at 6:00 p.m. and was not lifted until 6:00 a.m. the next day. But many people were at work or school or just outside when the curfew abruptly went into effect. My brother—who didn't fit the description of anyone the news broadcasted as storming the Capitol—was stopped and issued a warning. He told me that, not for the first time, he felt like he was being picked on by law enforcement because he is a Black man. Both my uncle and my brother had received versions of The Talk, and they lived to share their stories, but think about the trauma, among other things, borne out of those experiences.

I come to The Talk with a unique profile, qualifications, experiences, and interactions with law enforcement. My perspective on what to do when stopped by law enforcement is informed by this unique vantage point and knowledge. First, we'll discuss the fundamentals for all ages. Then, I go into some more "inside" tips, for teens and adults, on what you might say or do—and what not to say or do—when stopped.

I wouldn't be a good lawyer if I didn't include some disclaimers, caveats, and qualifiers before I dive in—you know, the fine print that lawyers love. This is *my* take on the system. My thoughts can never be a substitute for your views, judgment, and experience.

If hearing my uncle's and brother's stories is triggering or you feel like you have posttraumatic stress disorder (PTSD) or some other trauma associated with law enforcement, you are not alone. We, especially Black people, have collective trauma from seeing tragic images and hearing countless stories of unarmed Black people being killed at the hands of law enforcement. I know that every time I hear about another death of a Black boy, I hold my sons a little bit closer, I limit their social outings and exposure to the news, and I pray that things will be better (read: safer) during their lifetime. I, too, have ongoing concerns for my children. This talk cannot address every situation or even guarantee safe passage for you or your children. But it will be useful in many situations.

The Talk is my way to educate my kids on the dos and don'ts of interacting with law enforcement. Without knowing the specifics of what you are stepping into when you interact with law enforcement, I can offer only general advice. It is based on knowing what I know about how the police think and wanting to keep my sons—and your sons and daughters—safe.

THE BASICS

Every time I have to give my sons The Talk, despite the sobering topic, I remember Langston Hughes's poem "Mother to Son." The poem focuses on a mother encouraging her son to keep climbing and to never give up, no matter how difficult life gets. She tells her son that life hasn't been easy for her, but that he can overcome any obstacle because she has, and she continues to climb.

The poem is a monologue, but to me, The Talk is more of a dialogue, depending on the age of your child. I take the same approach as this fictitious mother in Hughes's poem. I adopt a tone of encouragement. I stress the importance of listening and understanding the instructions of The Talk. Then, I tell them to show me what they would do while I pretend to be the police officer. I borrowed this "show me" approach from the civil rights movement when four college students in 1960 prepared to conduct a nonviolent sit-in at a F. W. Woolworth store. The students prepared for the verbal and physical abuse that they would endure from the segregationists by subjecting themselves to simulations of that abuse in advance.

1. **Identify in advance an "in case of emergency" person who could be helpful if you are stopped by the police.** If your mother is a teacher, your father is in the military, your brother is a pastor, your grandfather is a lawyer, your neighbor is a firefighter, or if you know a cop—that information may be useful for the police to know, and I encourage you to tell them.

2. **Call someone.** Tell the police you would like to call your mother, father, sister, brother, best friend, or some other representative who could be helpful to this situation. Try to get them on the phone.

3. **Talk slowly and don't move.** Any sudden moves could make the police think you are a threat to them. It's best to speak slowly and stay still. Above all, DO NOT RUN. It seems obvious to say, but just in case.

4. **Comply with their instructions.** For example, if they tell you to turn your music down or off, now isn't the time to tell them that the music isn't loud.

5. **Tell them that you are complying with their instructions.** Narrate what you are doing as you do it (i.e., "I am putting my hands on the dash as you instructed").

6. **Keep your hands where the police can see them.** Don't reach into the glove compartment, the center console, your pockets, or bags without being instructed to do so. You don't

want the police officer to assume you have a gun or other weapon and react to a perceived threat.

7. **Do not give extraneous information** (we'll discuss this more later).

8. **Be respectful even when they disrespect you.** The police might yell at you; they might be aggressive with you or your property; they might interrupt you when you are talking. Even though this is frustrating, do not poke the bear. Say "Yes, ma'am" and "Yes, sir" and don't yell back.

9. **Humanize the police to be humanized by them** (more on this later).

10.   **Don't give them any reason to fear you.** This is a catchall statement. Use your best judgment, and control what you can. I recognize that they might just fear your skin, your voice, your height, and your overall Blackness—all things that you cannot control.

These are the essentials. And ground zero for any negotiations when you are the target.

PERSONALIZING YOUR TALK

Do you give The Talk, or some version of it, to your kids or someone you care about? What do you say? I know a mom who told her teenage son to inform the police up front that he is autistic so that the cops will be on notice. A client told me that he tells his son to tell the police right away that he has asthma and might need to get his inhaler out of his pocket, so that the police officer won't think that he is reaching for a weapon when he is getting his inhaler.

In your culture, what is your version of The Talk? Is it more general than how to behave with law enforcement? Is it how to act in public? With authority figures? With people of a certain race or ethnicity?

DIFFERENT AGES, DIFFERENT TALKS

Under Ten

When giving The Talk to children under the age of ten, you can liken it to the game Simon Says. Simon Says is a game in which the person playing the role of Simon gives instructions to the other players to perform physical actions. In the game, you have to do the actions only if Simon says "Simon says" before the action. You lose if you do what Simon commands if he didn't say "Simon says" first. In interactions with the police, the police officer is Simon, and the "Simon says" part is always implied. You want to do everything that Simon tells you to do and only what Simon tells you to do and nothing else.

Preteens

When giving The Talk to preteens, you want to impress upon them that police officers will often think they are older and more mature than their age might convey. This means you should continue to play Simon Says but recognize that you are no longer seen as a cute kid and that your perceived threat level to the cops is in a higher category. Tell them your age. Respect the uniform. You don't want to give them a reason or justification for taking your life. The game reference here is Truth or Dare. In that game, players have the choice of answering a question truthfully or performing a dare. With the police, you always want to choose truth. Answer their questions truthfully. Never perform the dare (e.g., trying to outmaneuver, outwit, or outrun the police).

Teenagers

When giving The Talk to teenagers, you want to share the stark reality that this may be the time of their life when the police perceive their threat to them as high. You continue to follow Simon Says, choose truth from Truth or Dare, and now, as a teenager, play a game of chess. Bluntly stated, you are the Black pawn and the police is the white king, but you don't want to win this game. To win in chess, you want to corner the king so he has no more moves, putting him in checkmate. You, as the pawn, want to stay on the board. That's your only goal. It is OK to lose this game if it means staying alive. The broader message here is: lose the battle, win the war. This means you can get a lawyer, file a claim, and seek justice later.

I don't think any of this abovementioned advice is easy to do or intuitive. Trust me. The Talk is something that Black parents wish we didn't have to give our kids, but it is necessary to protect them and to do what we can do to keep our kids safe. This is the advice that I give to my sons.

And by the way, you don't have to treat every police officer as if they will try to harm you. I grew up with and around the police. I know that most people become police officers to help and not harm people. In his stand-up comedy special *Tamborine*, Chris Rock refers to cops who are involved in police brutality as the "bad apples." Rock then goes on to say that there are just some professions (like police officers and airplane pilots) in which we cannot have bad apples. He is right. Full stop. But the reality is that there are some things you can control and some things that you cannot in your interactions with law enforcement. Of course, there is a presumption inherent in this chapter that we will not be able to cure in any one encounter with law enforcement all the discrimination, racism, sexism, homophobia, and so on embedded in the system. This chapter is about how to address the officers who have more in common with us than we may see when we look at their uniform and badge; it is about how to behave with the "good apples." Just like every tool that you are filling your toolbox with in this book, you have to determine the best way to utilize this information.

Remember that in dealing with the police, even the best ones, the threat level may be high—on both sides. Your first goal is to reduce THEIR sense that you are a high-level threat to them. By helping them see you are harmless, you are reducing the threat to yourself. Some police officers, like you, may be someone's mother, father, son, daughter, sister, or brother who just wants to make it home safely at the end of the night. I know that was always my dad's goal.

THE ADVANCED TALK

Now that we've gone over the basics, here's some advice for the more mature listener—and even yourself. The first goal is to keep calm. It will help you remember everything you need to do.

Keep Calm and Breathe

I know what you're thinking. When in the history of the world has someone said, "Stay calm," and that worked to actually calm the listener down? Or when has someone used that open hand gesture to indicate "relax" and effectively de-escalated heightening tensions? Look, I was outnumbered by at least eight armed men who entered my apartment to arrest Kevin, and I managed to stay calm, so I know you can do it, too.

First, breathe. Turning your attention to what you can control, focus on your breathing. Research shows that controlling your breathing is the most effective and fastest way to initiate a relaxation response in your body, which helps you think more clearly and leads to better performance under pressure. Two special breathing techniques that can help us stay calm are box breathing and tactical breathing.

Box breathing is used to return breathing back to a normal pace during or after a stressful experience. This is how you do it. Inhale through your nose for four seconds. Hold it for four seconds. Exhale out of your mouth for four seconds. Hold your breath for four seconds. The 4×4×4×4 corresponds to the four seconds for each step and is what gives you the visual of a box or square. The key here is to focus on filling and depleting the air in your lungs during the respective inhale and exhale. You can do this for as long as you need to, and you can make any necessary adjustments to your box (e.g., 2×2×2×2, holding for two seconds each). This technique is used not only by the US Navy SEALs but also other branches of the military, police officers, medical professionals, and other people in stressful situations. Why? Research shows that it focuses the mind, relieves stress, and helps you remain present and concentrate.

If box breathing focuses on your lungs, tactical breathing is chest and stomach breathing. In tactical breathing, you want to put your hand on your stomach and inhale while focusing on filling your stomach with air and exhale while focusing on emptying the air in your stomach. You can inhale for the same amount of time or you can inhale for four seconds and exhale for eight seconds. Research shows that this type of deep, rhythmic breathing can reduce anxiety, lessen anger responses, and, like box breathing, help you remain calm.

I use these breathing techniques in negotiations all the time, and you can, too. In my scenario with the FBI et al., my heart was pounding and racing. But I knew I had to calm my body down. When I have to advocate for my kids, my siblings, my friends, or my clients, I want to present from a place of power, and staying calm is the first step. I once had opposing counsel scream at me for about four minutes, and I used that time to box breathe because I saw his outburst as a strategy to disarm me. On the inside I was a mess, but on the outside, I was able to remain calm.

One of the key messages I give my sons is to stay calm even

when they perceive what is happening to them as unfair. I also tell them to be respectful even when they are being disrespected. In your negotiations, unfair things will happen. You may encounter people who do not share your same views on what respect looks and feels like. Employing these breathing techniques will help you stay calm.

Create Space / Tranquilize Chaos

The minute the men crowded into my studio apartment that early morning in DC, I knew measured breathing alone wouldn't be enough to stay calm. I needed more space—to breathe, and to think. To process what the guy in charge—let's call him Max— was about to tell me.

I was extremely aware of the other agents and officers putting Kevin in handcuffs and taking him away. I told you the place was pretty small. So after quickly assessing what was happening, I saw an opportunity to take some control. I seized it.

"Do you think some of the guys can leave now?" I asked. "You are taking Kevin. It's just me here now, and it is starting to feel a little too crowded. What do you think?"

The guys exchanged a look of surprise by my request, then one of them muttered, "She's right."

Everyone shifted to leave and head toward the door.

One of my first requests of the officers was to have some of them leave the apartment so that Max and I had more space to talk. Why is it helpful to create physical space when you are the target of police inquiry? Well, it may be obvious, but it is important to recognize that being a target or being in proximity to the target of a police action is an extremely stressful situation. If you open up space in the conversation and in the environment, then you will be in a better position to negotiate. I liken creating space in a negotiation to decluttering your home. Research shows that decluttering your environment helps your brain focus. In other words, the chaos competes for your attention. Addressing the chaos, especially after you have calmed yourself down, will help you concentrate and be sharp, productive, and effective. Second, your perception of what is happening to you and around you will be sharper.

Creating physical space can take many forms. You can create space by moving away from a table if you are seated or taking a step back if you are standing. Studies have shown that creating space, and especially green space, can help alleviate mental stress, anxiety, and depression. Sometimes you have a choice in the negotiation environment, and other times you don't. When the representatives from the four agencies were in my apartment, I wanted them out. I asked them if they would leave, and they did. That may not always be possible.

Take a Minute to Think and Interrupt Patterns

Take a minute to think. Whether you are the intended target or not, you need to create space in your mind. This concept comes from mindfulness practice and being present. The application in a negotiation is simple. You want to interrupt a pattern of escalation, and you also want to open up the mental space to think clearly about your options and what to do next. Pattern interruptions, through questions, or redirecting, can open up the space you need. Some people can think, self-reflect, and process on the spot. Others may need time. Another reason to interrupt patterns is to give law enforcement an opportunity to engage in cognitive reappraisal. Cognitive reappraisal is when someone changes how they are viewing a situation or appraising it.

In my situation, the threat to the police was stabilized once they left with the person they were there to take. They went in with the expectation that they might encounter a threat. Kevin's compliance and my nonthreatening behavior prompted them to reappraise the situation. And gave me further time to think about how to proceed.

Here are some examples of what you can say:

"I need to think."

"Give me a minute."

"I need a minute of silence to think."

"I need a few moments to process what's happening."

Asking the men to leave my apartment gave me space to think. I realized that I just needed to get Max, the main law enforcement officer who seemed to be engaging with me, talking. Granted, my personal threat level was down from a 10 to a 5, but I was still laser focused on staying alive. I recall thinking, *He won't shoot me if he doesn't think I am a threat to him*—and I wasn't.

Ask Questions

In my FBI situation, I asked questions until I felt as though there was no longer a threat to me. As the men filed out the door of my tiny studio apartment, I asked, "Before you go, can one of you tell me what is going on here? Should I call my dad? He's MPD."

All personnel left, except for Max. He said he could tell me what brought them to my doorstep in the first place. Point Damali. OK. Breathe, girl. I was no longer outmanned, even though I was still outgunned. I was hopeful I could bridge that gap by not being outsmarted.

I had asked the extra men to leave the apartment so that we had more space. Now, as my mind started to clear, I asked Max to fill me in. When he began to explain how Kevin had come under suspicion and what brought them there that day, I continued to ask for more details about why they were there with so many agencies and the threat they thought Kevin posed.

When you open space in a conversation, you slow things down enough to give yourself a chance to think. What is the best way to do this? Two words—ask questions. Asking questions forces you to deliberate on the proper question to ask. And it forces the other person to think about what they want to say. Asking questions makes both people more thoughtful and deliberate in their responses. Note that your inquiries should be open-ended because that is how you will get the most information (and it will also prevent you from speaking too much until you have a good sense of what is happening).

Examples of questions are:

"Can someone tell me what's going on?"
"Can you tell me why you stopped me?"
"What brings you here today?"

Figure Out What You Are Suspected Of (If You Can)

I have emphasized throughout the book the importance of knowing what you want in every negotiation, which often equates to figuring out your goal(s). When you are the target of the police, I'd say that more important than figuring out your goal, which ultimately is always going to be survival, is to figure out *what they suspect you of.* Obviously, every situation is different. And thus, your goal may differ accordingly. But first and foremost, it's helpful to know what their suspicions are, as again, it goes directly to your strategy—and to lowering the threat level.

After the men left my apartment, Max explained that following the terrorist attacks on the US on September 11, 2001, the Department of Homeland Security had increased surveillance at all bridges, tunnels, and ports. He then took out several photos of the Baltimore Harbor. Two photos in, I saw photos of Kevin's car and his license plate in clear view. Each photo was date and time stamped.

Max told me that a few days before, Kevin's car had been flagged as suspicious because it was parked at the Baltimore Harbor for three hours. No one got out of or into the car. Kevin had a friend visiting from his home country, a country that had been flagged on many watch lists, including the Office of Foreign Assets Control's sanctions list, as a country to watch for human rights violations and possible terrorist activity. Kevin and his friend visiting from abroad had not seen each other since they were teenagers. They drove to the harbor from DC and then sat in the car catching up for hours. To them, it was a stroll down memory lane. To the FBI, it looked like they were terrorists surveilling a possible target.

When they checked the car's license plate, it showed it was registered to Kevin, who had entered the US legally on a tourist visa but who had never left. He had overstayed his visa by about ten years. And because Kevin was from a country that the US had flagged, his casual catch-up with a visiting countryman quickly aroused suspicion, making him public enemy number one. Mind you, I did not know any of the details surrounding Kevin's immigration status until Max told me. My jaw dropped as I tried to process all the information, but I urged Max to tell me more.

I now knew a few things: I knew what Kevin was suspected of. And why they came to my home. This helped me know how to proceed. If you know what you are suspected of, it can be invaluable in regard to what information you offer up and what information you don't. You do not want to offer random information.

Do Not Give Extraneous Information

One thing to know up front: the police rarely enter any negotiation with a blank slate. In target situations, they are not peeking inside your bag to get to know you better so that you can develop a rapport. Most often, they have a single goal in mind: to get evidence that they can then use to support their arrest and provide evidence for a prosecutor's case against you. So when they ask you questions, they are asking those questions with a purpose—to determine whether they think you are guilty of a crime.

This is why you often hear the advice that you should just say nothing. Because the last thing you want to do is to inadvertently incriminate yourself by speaking to the wrong assumption or giving information that the police or a prosecutor can use against you.

For a lighter illustration, there is a hilarious scene in the movie *There's Something about Mary* in which Ben Stiller's character is brought in for questions about a murder, but Ben Stiller thinks that he is being interrogated about picking up a hitchhiker. The detectives ask him a very open-ended question: "How many are we talking here?" In their minds they are clearly asking about how many murders he has committed. Ben Stiller's character responds, "I don't know. Twenty-five. Fifty. I mean, who keeps track?" He believes the cops are asking about the number of hitchhikers he has given rides to over the years. The officers immediately seize on his answer as proof that he is indeed a murderer. This is a movie and not real, but I see situations like this happen regularly where communication leads to misunderstandings, and people inadvertently incriminate themselves.

There is a reason that we have Miranda rights in the US, and some version of these reminders of self-incrimination exists in other jurisdictions. In the US, Miranda rights can vary from state to state, but typically they are usually some variations of these four sentences:

1. You have the right to remain silent.
2. Anything you say can and will be used against you in a court of law.
3. You have a right to an attorney.
4. If you cannot afford an attorney, one will be appointed for you.

The Miranda warning is designed to help someone suspected of a crime invoke their Fifth Amendment rights under the US Constitution. I refer to these rights in this chapter to remind you that your goal in this situation is not to give extraneous information or even to give information to get information as discussed in chapter 4.

If appropriate, ask questions to figure out what you're suspected of and allay their suspicions accordingly. But answer questions only if you are sure that your responses will lower tensions rather than escalate them. And that you are not incriminating yourself. One way to do this is to limit the information that you share.

When You're Innocent, Share Three Details

When many of us encounter law enforcement, we want something *not* to happen. We don't want to be arrested or detained. Heck, we even want to avoid getting that speeding ticket. So our first impulse is to prove we are innocent. All of these are valid goals. Again, the first step is to understand what you are being accused of and to not give out incriminating information.

Assuming the threat level has been lowered, it can be useful to offer appropriate pieces of information about your actions or situation. I often recommend giving the police three specific details that could help you. Here are some examples.

I have been pulled over for driving above the speed limit, and because my goal was to avoid a ticket and still try to make it to my destination on time, I've offered up that I was speeding to pick up my kid, that I usually don't speed, and, depending on the officer's mood, something slightly humorous like, "I totally would have slowed down if I knew you were hiding in the cut."

I have been interviewed by the police after I was in a car accident where I was rear-ended, and my goal was for the police officer to determine that I was not at fault so that the cost of my car insurance would not increase. In that case I told them I have photos of the accident. I brought forward two witnesses who were in the car with me at the time who could support my story.

And I made sure to mention that the person who hit me admitted that it was his fault when he hopped out of the car and said, "Hey, sorry, that was totally my fault. I wasn't paying attention."

Once I was stopped by the police while I was walking across the park with three friends in Nagoya, Japan. I was the only person stopped because, as I was told directly by the policeman, "Black people from different countries sell drugs in this park." My goal was to not get arrested. I explained that I was in Japan because I was a student at Nagoya University of Foreign Studies. I mentioned that I was American and not from the countries that the officers mentioned. Finally, I told them why I was crossing the park—to get to the train station—and gave them the name of the restaurant where we had dinner nearby and identified the train station we were going to on the other side of the park.

Sometimes it is important to speak up. My advice is to share your status or something about you with the police to dispel their belief that you did or are in the process of doing something wrong. Make sure that whatever you are sharing is relevant to your goal. In the Japan example above, I chose the three details I shared with the police specifically to help dispel their theory that I was selling drugs in the park. The point here is to not just say "I'm innocent" but to use the three details to show them that you are.

Humanize Them to Be Humanized

This is probably the hardest piece of advice, especially if someone is treating you in a way that is dehumanizing. Former US First Lady Michelle Obama coined the catchphrase "When they go low, we go high" in 2016 at the Democratic National Convention.

She said, "When someone is cruel or acts like a bully, you don't stoop to their level. No, our motto is: When they go low, we go high." Ms. Obama acknowledged in her book *The Light We Carry* that going high is hard to do. To me, trying to humanize someone when you are being dehumanized, or worse, not even being seen as or treated as human, is the ultimate test of whether you can go high when they are going low. How can you humanize someone so that they can humanize you?

These are the things that I think of when trying to humanize someone else in a negotiation, conflict, or police interaction. I consider:

- how the other person is human
- how they are complex like me
- how they have their own life stories
- how they may have invisible challenges
- how maybe the way they are interacting with me comes from a prior situation that had nothing to do with me, but they are taking it out on me

Once Max and I were alone, it was easier to humanize him. He was giving me the information I asked for. He really didn't mean me any harm. The threat level to me dropped even further as he finished his story of why they were arresting Kevin.

Kevin's "suspicious" behavior at the harbor had quickly made his detention and deportation a priority for law enforcement. And because of all the various issues in question, four agencies were involved. Though of course their conclusions about Kevin being a terrorist were wrong, I could see where Max and the others were coming from on his immigration status. Max's explanation made sense.

By staying to tell me what had brought the agencies to my home, Max became human to me. When he left, all my fear and anxiety about my situation dissipated. Of course, I was still worried about what was going to happen to Kevin, but at least I no longer feared for my life. The version of The Talk that my parents had given to me kept me alive. Kevin, also alive after this encounter, was safely deported to his country.

My parents gave me The Talk circa 1988. I am still giving my kids this advice in 2023. I told you that versions of The Talk have been happening for generations. I look forward to the day when The Talk is no longer needed. In the meantime, I hope you craft your personalized version to put into your tool kit.

NEGOTIATION IRL TOOL KIT

The Talk—The Basics

- Identify in advance an "in case of emergency" person who could be helpful if you are stopped by the police.
- Call someone.
- Talk slowly and don't move.
- Comply with their instructions.
- Tell them that you are complying with their instructions.
- Keep your hands where the police can see them.

- Do not give extraneous information.
- Be respectful even when they disrespect you.
- Humanize the police to be humanized by them.
- Don't give them any reason to fear you.

The Advanced Talk

- Remain calm and breathe. Try 4×4×4×4 box breathing.
- Create space in the conversation or environment to tranquil-ize the chaos around you or inside your head.
- Take a minute to think and interrupt patterns of escalation.
- Ask (open-ended) questions.
- Know your Miranda rights.
     1. You have the right to remain silent.
     2. Anything you say can and will be used against you in a court of law.
     3. You have a right to an attorney.
     4. If you cannot afford an attorney, one will be appointed for you.
- Figure out what you are suspected of.
- Do not give extraneous information.
- Share three details to help dispel the police's belief of wrong-doing when you are innocent.
- Humanize them to be humanized.

8.

Know Your Kryptonite

How to Manage Your Emotional Triggers in a Negotiation

I sat paralyzed, completely in shock, mouth agape. I couldn't believe what I was seeing.

As a corporate transactional attorney, I was always in some stage of negotiating, and today had started off no differently. I was in my home office preparing for several ongoing negotiations, and was a bit stir-crazy to boot. We were two months into the COVID-19 pandemic, and like most people back then, I was always inside and desperate to go out. Until, that is, that morning, when I saw a video on my iPhone that made me want to remain indoors indefinitely. Not to mention, I wanted to pull into my arms every Black man I knew, especially my husband, my two sons, my father, and my five brothers. I feared for their lives and all Black lives, really.

I'm not much of a crier. Never have been. It's just how I am built. My job requires me to sit in the middle of conflict all day, so professionally, my lack of this normal emotional response comes in handy. Don't get me wrong; I am loving, caring, and empathic. I feel pain, and I am human. I just don't cry—not even when everyone around me is crying. Not even at funerals. But the tears were now streaming down my face as I watched the murder of forty-six-year-old George Floyd under the knee of a white male police officer.

What could this man, who looked exactly like half of the men in my family and had a particularly striking resemblance to my six-foot-eight younger brother whom I call "gentle giant," have done to warrant his public execution? The details of what led to his arrest were still being revealed, but what was immediately apparent just from watching the video was that he did not resist arrest, and that he told the cop, who continuously pressed his knee down on Floyd's neck for approximately eight minutes and forty-six seconds, that he could not breathe. George Floyd himself said it over twenty times. As did the onlookers. He couldn't breathe. You didn't need any medical training to see Floyd was in distress. It was right there on the video. I kept watching, and as the tears continued to flow, my stomach tied into knots and the anxiety started to kick in. Oh my . . . is he going to die? Is his light about to be extinguished? All his dreams deferred? What did he do to deserve this?

The news reported that Floyd had paid for cigarettes at a local store with a counterfeit twenty-dollar bill. What? The store clerk called the police, and seventeen minutes after the police answered the call, George Floyd was dead. Over a twenty-dollar bill. And cigarettes. The tears stopped. I was angry. No, what's stronger than anger? I was apoplectic. So you're telling me that a Black man's life is worth less than a pack of cigarettes? The thought that the police could publicly engage in a modern-day lynching left me raw with fury. I was furious that our Black men were not safe. Livid that no one had stepped up to help Floyd or stop his execution. Infuriated that one man could wield so much power over another man. And incensed that even though I had devoted the last few years of my life to training hundreds of New York police officers how to de-escalate conflict with their words instead of weapons following the murder of Eric Garner, whose famous last words were "I can't breathe," the people we relied on to protect us could do this—again. How could it be that in Minnesota, Georgia, Wisconsin, Kentucky, and a slew of other states, unarmed Black men and women were still not safe when they bought cigarettes, went out for a run, slept at home, walked from a convenience store, fell asleep in a car, sat in their car, stood in Grandma's backyard, played at the playground, sat in their living room, and just woke up Black?

Sadness overcame me as I saw George Floyd take his last breath and call out to his mother, to his children, and then declare himself dead. He pronounced his own death before the paramedics did. Who wants to live in a world where this could happen? Like so many Black parents, like so many people in general, like each of you, I had worked so hard with so many sleepless nights to make the world a better place for my Black sons. I had sacrificed to send them to good schools and live in safe neighborhoods. I tried to broaden their horizons by showing them the world (by the ages of six and nine, respectively, they had been to over forty states and thirty countries). I had already given them an age-appropriate version of The Talk, with dos and don'ts to guide their interactions with the police, as discussed in chapter 7.

But what was it all for, if at any moment the police could just take their life? I felt hopeless and helpless. I needed to *feel* as if I could protect myself. To protect my family. To protect Black people. To protect Brown people. To protect anyone who has been oppressed or marginalized. To protect anyone from having their potential cut short or anyone who had been underestimated. Yet I felt like there was nothing that I could do, despite my best efforts, my education, my experience, and my access.

The day I watched the video of George Floyd's murder, I was so triggered that I felt a flood of emotions inside. Outside, I was also facing quite a conundrum. It was well known in many circles that I trained NYPD officers, that my dad was a policeman (retired by that time), and that I had many friends within the police department in various ranks across all five boroughs of New York City. Within hours of the Floyd video going viral, all hell broke loose, and the world took to the streets to protest. In those rallies, allies were getting hurt, my Black people were getting hurt, and my cops were getting hurt. It was a colossal mess.

Meanwhile, back in New York City, both the police and my community thought I could clean up at least some of it. Only if I stood with them. *Say something inspirational, Damali*, they said. *You are a conflict resolution expert. Fix this. Help us. Tell them that we are not all the same. Tell them that we are not all bad, Damali.*

Wait . . . , I thought. *Who do you want me to speak for? Black people or cops? Which side?*

As in most high-conflict situations, including high-conflict negotiations, the initial division is an "us" versus "them" scenario. The sentiment is that you are either with us or against us. There is no in between. By force, design, or silence—you have to pick a side. So what was I going to do? Was I going to support the police and stand with them? (Let's not forget that I was raised by a stay-at-home mom, and it was a police officer's salary that fed and clothed us and kept a roof over our heads.) Or was I going to grab a protest sign and stand with my people, my people who had had enough of being victimized by police brutality?

I asked myself: *Did I bleed blue, or did I bleed black?*

TAKE A STEP BACK

I needed a minute.

When you are triggered—and in negotiations, you may frequently be triggered—take a step back. It's the first piece of advice I always give. Remove yourself from the situation, and put space and time in between you and the triggering event. Take a break. "Go to the balcony," as negotiation experts Fisher and Ury would say. Put on your own oxygen mask before you help others, as they say in the safety instructions on the airplane. Whatever version of the advice resonates most with you, do it. Focus on yourself first and protect your peace. Creating space when you are feeling flooded is often the initial step to managing those feelings, processing them, and releasing them.

The process of managing your emotional triggers in a negotiation resembles the process of managing your triggers in everyday life. *Especially* when it comes to taking a step back. If you are arguing with your romantic partner and your buttons are pushed, go to another room and meditate. I know people who keep a mindfulness app on their phone for this very purpose. If you and your parents or siblings are rehashing the same old political debate, say you are going for a walk and get out of there. If you can't take a walk outside, excuse yourself for at least a bathroom break.

If you are on the phone with a friend and she is still nagging you about not making it to her thirtieth birthday party and she is fifty-seven years old, tell her a call is coming through on your other line and get off the phone. Then do some deep breathing.

And if your local police precinct wants to know if you are going to publicly stand with them while people globally are protesting police brutality, and Black people want to know if you are going to stand with them because you woke up Black that morning and remained Black throughout the day and into the night—create some space. You don't have to respond immediately. And I didn't.

Here's what I did instead: I took an online yoga class. Don't you dare judge me! It was COVID times, I needed a break, and hey, no one was taking classes in person—even my youngest son, who was in kindergarten, was learning how to color online! Another thing I did to pause and de-escalate during those stressful times: I watched a ton of comedy specials online. I needed shows that would make me laugh, because the world was literally burning around me, and even with all my training, I couldn't handle it—at least not at the moment. Instead of talking, I listened and I laughed. I watched comedians Dave Chappelle, Sam Morril, Sebastian Maniscalco, Rachel Feinstein, Ali Wong, Wanda Sykes, and Jo Koy. I may not have been able to fix what was happening in the world at that moment, but thanks to Jo Koy, I was able to diagnose my husband's sleep apnea.

And you know what else I did during those emotionally uncertain times? I thought about writing my first-ever book proposal. I faced a lot of pressure from both my police friends and my Black community to "stand with them," but something about their requests, to me, felt like a short-term solution, like a

Band-Aid. Just standing in solidarity for standing's sake was not going to address the core problems of a system that was broken and a relationship that was toxic. It wasn't going to address implicit and explicit bias. Or how to negotiate in the face of that bias. And it wasn't going to tell us what to do when triggered, or how to process the trauma. Maybe there was another way.

Everyone wanted me to pick a side. What I needed, however, was to process how I was feeling and assess what I needed to do. I am still trying to process how I feel about all this. I was afraid, anxious, angry, and sad, and you know what? I wasn't alone.

Two reputable surveys highlighted the psychological impact of Floyd's death using data collected prior to his death and in the week following his death using two population surveys. The Gallup survey showed unprecedented levels of sadness and anger affecting more than one-third of the US population, with Black people showing the highest increases. The other survey, Household Pulse, conducted by the US Census Bureau, showed that Black Americans had significantly higher rates of depression and severe anxiety than white Americans. When you are feeling like this, you don't know what to do or what to do first. Sometimes the best thing to do is nothing (at least at first) until you know with a clear mind what to do.

It was morning when I saw the George Floyd video, and I still had three negotiation calls remaining. I knew that I was in no position to perform at my best given all the emotions I was experiencing. I needed to take a step back, create space, and protect my peace. I set a healthy boundary and communicated it. I sent a quick message to my counterparts on the upcoming calls that simply said, "Need to reschedule. Something came up." Not a single person complained, pushed back, or refused my request. And by the way, my email to my counterparts wasn't a request. Note I did not write, "Can we reschedule?" I was not interested in whether my need to take a step back was OK with them. I did not need their permission or buy-in to take time to focus on my self-care, and you don't need that either when you are triggered. This is one of those situations that, as the saying goes, was "better to ask for forgiveness than to ask for permission."

Regardless of whether you are triggered before a negotiation or while negotiating, ask yourself if you can do your job to the best of your ability given the circumstances. If the answer is no or even "I'm not sure," then do not negotiate at that time. Instead, take the time you need before reengaging.

Once you've taken a step back and possibly set a boundary, the next step is to acknowledge your emotions.

ACKNOWLEDGE YOUR EMOTIONS

Until recently, negotiation books didn't take a deep dive into how emotions impact the negotiation process. The approach was more transactional, less focused on the psychological lens. Yet using your emotional intelligence will improve the chances of getting what you want and what you need.

Old negotiation advice used to tell you to have a poker face. In some cases, that might still be helpful. We'll get to the need not to be reactive shortly. What you shouldn't do is ignore your own emotions. Everyone, even seasoned negotiators, experiences emotions during conflict. You can gather as much information about the other person—and the negotiation—as possible. You can learn the process of negotiation, know your subject matter inside and out, and prepare for interactions with the people involved, but you also must prepare for being triggered and the emotions that may bubble up as a result. Be ready to identify your emotions and "stay ready," as my paternal grandfather used to say.

Why is it so important to acknowledge and name emotions? Because the more quickly you can name your emotions, the easier it is to regulate them. If we are aware of what emotion we are feeling—say, sadness or frustration—we are better able to lessen and release that emotion, especially with practice. The goal is to become so skilled at detailing and understanding your emotions and triggers that you can avoid any negative or harmful behaviors associated with them, such as blowups in the boardroom or with a negotiation counterpart.

Watching the George Floyd video, I felt sadness, anxiety, and anger, but my predominant emotion was fear. I feared for George Floyd's life. And as I watched him take his last breath, I feared for the life of my brother who most resembled Floyd and for my other four brothers. I feared for my dad, my uncles, and all my male cousins scattered throughout the US. And in New York, I feared for my young sons. But I feared the most for my husband.

I was terrified that the police, during this particular time period, would pull my husband over while he was driving and kill him. One night, my husband told me that he was going to drive into New York City the next day to run some basic errands. We had temporarily moved out of our apartment in Manhattan, opting for more space upstate during the coronavirus lockdown, and he wanted to check in on it. I pleaded with him not to go. I shared with him my fears about him getting pulled over by the police and something really bad happening during a particularly contentious time between police officers and civilians.

I had been in contact with some of the officers that I had trained, and I learned that given the COVID-19 pandemic, many cops were out sick or in quarantine. To make up for the thinner ranks, those still working had twelve-hour shifts instead of eight-hour shifts—mandatory overtime—and they were allowed only one day off instead of two. So when everything was popping off against the police, NYPD officers were overworked, overtired, getting assaulted, and being threatened with being defunded.

Nope. I was not letting my husband out of my sight. He told me that I was overreacting, and you know, maybe I was. But you couldn't convince me that I was wrong in my thinking. My husband is a Black man named Chad, and he graduated from Princeton and Georgetown Law. I knew he could take care of himself, but I couldn't get past my fear to let him take the chance.

Cautiously, I asked him what time he planned to head to the city in the morning. He told me 9:00 a.m., because there was still minimal traffic during the early days of the pandemic. I set my alarm for 5:00 a.m. When it rang, I rolled out of our bed and landed on the floor without making a sound. Ninja-like, I quietly sneaked out of our room. And once I was comfortably out of the house, I hopped in the car and drove to the city. We had only one car at the time, and I knew that if I took it and ran the city errands that Chad had mentioned, that he would have no reason to go to the city for a while. When he woke up a few hours later, he called me. Expecting the call, I answered on the first ring.

"Where did you go?" Chad asked.

"To the city," I said.

"Why?" he asked.

"Because I was too scared to let you go. I was worried that you wouldn't come back."

"D, the police can stop you, too," he said. His words made me think of Sandra Bland. He wasn't wrong. Point Chad.

"I know," I said. "But I am the daughter of a police officer. Plus, the closer I get to the city [we were staying an hour north of Manhattan at the time], I will be within the confines of the precincts where I trained many officers."

In other words, I knew what to say and what to do with the police if they stopped me because I am the daughter of a policeman. I am also a Black woman, not a Black man. In my mind, I had a slightly better chance at survival than Chad.

I don't think I realized it at the time, but Chad and I were in a real-life negotiation, and I wanted to win—to keep him safe. In retrospect, my behavior could have been viewed by outsiders as exasperating or even controlling. I left my own husband without a car! Without telling him. He might have gotten angry with me as well. But he didn't. Why? Because I had named my emotions—and so had he. I was acting out of fear and anxiety—and a desire to protect. And though in this case naming my emotions didn't stop me from acting without consultation, acknowledging and explaining the emotions did prevent any escalation or misunderstanding over what I'd done.

Being able to take a step back and acknowledge my emotions was also my first step in eventually releasing my fear—and not intervening when my husband had to drive into the city in the subsequent weeks and months. But again, I wasn't quite there yet.

Acknowledging your emotions in order to release them is important to do with your family and friends; it's also crucial during a negotiation. A blowup with your husband is one thing; a blowup with a counterpart could have even more severe consequences. But here's the thing: sometimes it's not even the outburst that can affect your chance of getting an optimal outcome. Sometimes it's your failure to acknowledge and thus deal with the emotion, period.

Take my friend Lauren. While I was still sorting out my emotions and feeling sad after the death of George Floyd, Lauren was in New York City feeling humiliated. Lauren is the senior business partner of a financial services company. She handles the day-to-day communications, negotiations, and management of a large team, and that month she'd been negotiating a deal with a team of international clients from Mexico, Holland, Brazil, Spain, and Ecuador. There was nothing she didn't know about the deal. She had been on 100 percent of the calls and in every meeting.

Her counterpart on the other side was named Dave. Lauren and Dave had the same professional rank, had the same amount of experience, and a similar education. They even both wore the same designer clothing brands—Hugo Boss suits, with Thomas Pink French cuff shirts and Ferragamo shoes. They were mirror images of each other except that Dave was a white man and Lauren was a Black woman.

On the penultimate day before their deal was executed, the parties all met in the conference room next to Lauren's office. Lauren and Dave took turns discussing the final steps on how to close. It was getting late in the evening and everyone was tired. Dave called out to Lauren in front of everyone, "Hey, Lauren, can you get coffee and order food for everyone?"

Lauren smiled outwardly, but on the inside she was mortified that he had asked her, the only woman and Black person on the team, to handle the food and drinks for everyone, especially since junior members of their teams were present. She wanted to say or do something, but she didn't know what to say or do. So Lauren took everyone's order and had food and drinks delivered.

From that moment onward, her confidence was shattered. If Lauren had been able to name her feelings of shame and embarrassment, she might have been able to release them. Instead, she shut down and tried to ignore them, which was probably the worst thing she could have done. Her interactions with Dave became suddenly tense. He had gotten under her skin. Thrown off her game, Lauren pushed back on a reasonable suggestion that would have also benefited her company because she was triggered and didn't know how to move on. She was harming her own deal due to her inability to acknowledge, name, and thus release her emotions.

Raise your hand if you have been triggered in a negotiation or conversation and you felt a series of emotions, or even just one dominant emotion. Like Lauren and me, you will be triggered at some point, and you will have an emotional reaction, and guess what? That is OK. It is OK. It is normal to feel sad and give yourself the space to feel sad. It is normal to feel angry when we are humiliated or underestimated. It is normal to feel anxious when you see someone being murdered by a person who is supposed to protect and serve. But I promise you that if you are able to acknowledge the emotions and name them, as opposed to ignoring and shutting them down, you will be able to release them more quickly and get on with what you are doing.

As Nedra Glover Tawwab, licensed therapist and author of *Set Boundaries, Find Peace*, says, "The hard truth: We don't get rid of feelings because we're tired of having them. Feelings go away once we accept them and we're no longer responding to the stimuli that created them."

So how do we better accept our feelings and stop responding to the stimuli so that we aren't harming our own deals as Lauren did? Along with naming and acknowledging our emotions, it can be helpful to become more familiar with our kryptonite.

KNOW YOUR KRYPTONITE: IDENTIFY YOUR TRIGGERS AND THE WHY

If you think about it, what do you have 100 percent control over in a negotiation? Yourself. Especially when dealing with someone more powerful (or someone who believes they are more powerful because they are underestimating you), the only thing you may be able to control is you. That, of course, is easier said than done.

The first step is to identify your triggers. Triggers are what set off our feelings and emotions. Common triggers in a negotiation are ideas, topics, or subjects that cause you to feel anxious, tense, afraid, apprehensive, ashamed, concerned, or angry. Just think about the last negotiation you were in. What was going on for you? What ticked you off?

Another helpful question to ask is: *Why* were you upset by whatever triggered you? When Dave asked Lauren to get the coffee and order the food, she might have asked herself why this was so triggering for her. She might then have been able to name that the emotion she was feeling was humiliation. And she might have connected that to all the other times she, as a Black woman, had been asked to do things that she felt were beneath her abilities and position. She might even have been able to see that it wasn't just Dave's request, but a whole history of requests, that was flooding her with emotion. Seeing the why can help us process— and cope with—the feeling.

Anger can be a cover-up for many other emotions. Sometimes

it helps to dig deeper, to get underneath the anger to see the true why, or the root of the trigger. Before the pandemic, a Black man I knew named Keith, a senior partner at a company, was preparing to transition to a new job. He had given his company the customary two weeks' notice, and he still had about a week to go. Keith was beloved by his junior colleagues, and unbeknownst to him, once he had given his notice, many of the people who reported to him decided to follow him out the door. To the company, it felt like a massive exodus from one of their most profitable departments and as if Keith had orchestrated the whole thing (he did not, by the way) in violation of the nonsolicitation provision in his separation agreement. The company did not even check with Keith to see whether he knew about the other people leaving the company. Instead, they sent two security officers up to tell him, in front of all his colleagues, that that day would be his last. Keith had worked at this company for over fifteen years. Yet here was security giving him fifteen minutes to pack up his personal belongings into whatever could fit into one small Bankers Box. He had to leave everything else behind, and the security guards escorted him out of the building.

You can probably guess that the emotion that bubbled up for Keith was anger. And he was angry. Instead of having the dignified exit he expected and deserved, he was being treated like a common criminal. A negotiation ensued between Keith and the lead security guard—let's call him Nathan—whom Keith had known for ten years. Following strict orders from the top, the lead security guard refused to negotiate with Keith. Keith asked for more time. Nathan refused. Keith asked for more boxes to pack his things. Nathan refused. Keith asked if he could have some privacy. Nathan had the other security guard stand outside Keith's office while Nathan remained inside with Keith. Seeing that on top of everything else that was happening—the negotiation with Nathan was going nowhere—sent Keith into a tailspin. As a result, he said some things on his way out that to this day he wished he hadn't said.

How many times have we said something in the heat of the moment or during a tense negotiation that we wish we could take back or that we hadn't said? I know that chapter 6 explores recovering from unintended offenses, but this is different. Here I am talking about understanding what sets you off, knowing your kryptonite, so that you do not commit the offense in the first place.

When Keith and I dug deeper into the why of Keith's negative emotions and triggered state, we uncovered the real reason he was angry. Sometimes when an emotion looks like anger, it is really fear, anxiety, shame, or a violation of dignity. Under the anger, Keith felt a loss of dignity. And that loss of dignity or face was a particular trigger for him. Knowing his kryptonite would not have changed the unpleasantness of that final day for Keith, but it did help him repair and move on from the relationships at his workplace that had been damaged by the words exchanged in his final encounters.

Knowing our kryptonite, or understanding our triggers, can also help us anticipate similar stimuli and thus incidents. If we see a pattern beginning to form, we can use that knowledge to head off future knee-jerk responses or shutdowns. As Glover Tawwab points out, "When you deny your feelings, there's no room for the feeling to be processed and released. Naming emotions facilitates processing and moving forward. Acknowledging the impact of a feeling also helps you recognize and prevent triggering situations in the future. You can only grow from situations when you learn from them."

REGULATE YOUR EMOTIONS

When you are in a negotiation, knowing how to regulate your emotions is as essential as mastering the subject matter of your deal and learning as much as you can about your counterpart—it is a part of your preparation. Once you know what your triggers are and have named your emotional responses, you are in a better position to prepare in advance for whatever triggers you. The goal is to recognize what's happening, know what to do, and how to calm yourself when you are provoked. Here is where emotional regulation comes into play.

Emotional regulation is when you put enough space between feeling the emotion and reacting to it. You may not be able to take a daylong break, or the longer time-out that I was able to take after the George Floyd incident, but even a short pit stop to collect your thoughts before you respond can help, as we saw with the bathroom breaks in the section "Take a Step Back." When we emotionally regulate, the space between emotion and reaction is even shorter: with practice, it may take only a split second to adjust our reaction to a trigger.

The ability to regulate your emotional reaction to an event helps you moderate your behavior. Studies show that neural mechanisms can help you downregulate, which means decreasing the intensity of a negative emotional response. In other words, if your initial response when triggered is a negative emotion, such as aggression, neural mechanisms—structures such as neurons, neural circuits, and regions of the brain that regulate emotional responses—can help you avoid an aggressive response. For example, someone who is triggered and becomes angry might yell. If they are able to regulate their emotion, however, they can choose another response that is not the predictable yelling. They might be able to retain their calm, or even smile, nonplussed by any attempts to ruffle their feathers.

Two common ways to practice emotional regulation are to use cognitive reappraisal and attention control. We explored cognitive reappraisal in chapter 6, which is when you reframe a problem to think about it in another way. An example of cognitive *appraisal* can be applied to Lauren's situation. Lauren felt humiliated when Dave asked her to order food for everyone because she thought Dave had singled her out because she was a woman and, perhaps, because she was a Black woman. Again, if Lauren had been able to name, process, and release her emotions more quickly, cognitive *reappraisal*, or reframing, might have led her to see Dave's ask as something a visitor/guest would customarily ask the host of a meeting, whether they were male or female, if they were working late and it was dinnertime. In other words, if Lauren had reframed the way she internalized Dave's request from a negative to something that was normal, she might have seen an alternate, nonhumiliating explanation for his behavior. And this revelation could have helped her come up with a more appropriate response than outwardly acquiescing while internally seething.

Once I pointed out to Lauren how she was harming her own deal because she had not regulated her emotions, she decided to test my theory during her next meeting with Dave and his deal team. Since she had acknowledged her emotions, she was prepared when it became late and Dave and his team were still sitting in her conference room. When Dave looked at her and said, "Coffee and dinner for the teams? Can you take care of it, Lauren?"

she was ready. She looked up from her computer, paused for a moment, and said, "Great minds think alike. I ordered from the same restaurant as before, placing the exact same order as before. Plus, I added some gluten-free, vegan, and dairy-free options for the new folks." Dave smiled and said, "That's why I like when you host our meetings. You always make us feel so welcome and you make it look effortless. We don't experience such good treatment with other deal teams. Thanks, Lauren." Lauren beamed inwardly and patted herself on the back for doing the work in the interim to acknowledge her emotions. Lauren went on to get everything she needed in that negotiation and most of what she wanted, too.

Attention control is another way to regulate your emotions when triggered. It is exactly what it sounds like. In the moment, it can be helpful to redirect your attention away from whatever triggered your emotional response. Studies in this area have primarily focused on pain and diverting someone's attention when they fall. Whether you are a parent or not, you may notice that you do this instinctively with kids, right? There is this split second when a kid falls where the kid looks up at you, before they have an outward expression of pain or shock. Feeling this moment, we say to the kid, "Get up, shake it off." In that moment, we divert their attention from the fall to getting up and shaking it all off maybe before they process the pain or shock from falling.

When we use attention control, we can divert from the negative. We can also divert to the positive. Here are two techniques you can try.

- *Repeat a mantra.* Say something three times. "I am not the target" is a mantra I repeated when the FBI came to my home in chapter 7. What would you have said to calm your-self down in that moment? Depending on the scenario, you might want to have three to six words that you can say when you need to calm down, redirect, or focus. When I am a mediator engaged in a facilitative process, I usually like to remind myself and my students that you do not have to fix the problem for the other person. You have to, instead, cre-ate the space for all sides to feel heard and encourage under-standing and, if possible, resolution. Some effective mantras to repeat to remind you are:

"It's not about you."
"You don't have to fix it."
"Remember why you are here."

■ *Have a response or comeback, ideally humorous, ready, locked, and loaded.* Just think of how Lauren might have been able to turn her situation around if she had been able to respond to the coffee request with a quick quip like, "Sure, but you know I make $750 an hour, so that's gonna be one expensive coffee." Rather than letting her embarrassment and the ten-sion in the room rule, she might have been able to make the atmosphere a bit more light-hearted, saving the situation—and her negotiation—then and there.

These emotional regulation tips may help you when you're in the middle of a negotiation and have to make a game-time deci-sion of what to do. With practice, these split-second pivots may become second nature for you. Perhaps they already are.

In the long term, however, especially if you are prone to emotional flooding, you may have to do more work. Here are some tips on how to better process your emotions over time:

- Make it a practice to name your emotions when you are feeling irritated or upset.
- Keep track of your triggers in a journal and register your emotional responses. Writing them down will help with the processing.
- Ask yourself why something triggered you. Write that down as well.
- Manage difficult feelings by processing and accepting them rather than minimizing or ignoring them.
- Define your boundaries: What do you not want to hear or say?
- Speak with a supportive person or a mental health professional.

Ultimately, what is important is to identify the emotion you are experiencing, acknowledge it, then accept the emotion and release it. Acknowledging and recognizing negative triggers and emotions helps you prevent triggering situations in the future. There are a few more ways that you can manage your emotional triggers so that you can focus on negotiating from a place of power.

TALK ABOUT IT

After the George Floyd video went viral, it seemed like everyone around me wanted to talk about it. Activists wanted to talk about mobilizing. Parents wanted to talk about protecting our kids. Allies called, texted, and wrote to tell me that they stood with me and wanted to talk about what they should do, what Black-owned businesses they should support, and which organizations they should donate to to support the cause.

What happened to George Floyd traumatized many people who watched the video or heard the story. And for those who already felt trauma around these types of incidents, the video triggered their trauma anew. Research shows that there are a lot of reasons to talk about trauma, with my favorite reasons coming from Dr. Ellen Hendriksen. According to Dr. Hendriksen, there are five reasons to talk about it: to find support, to get a reality check, to make sense of what happened, to realize that you are more than the trauma, and to make meaning out of what happened. While I was still processing the video, my initial reaction to being asked to choose a side between the police and Black people was to go to yoga, watch comedy shows, and sketch out my ideas for this book. But I eventually wanted to talk about it. You may want to talk about your trauma, too.

Find Support, Check Your Reality

There is something cathartic in knowing that you are not alone in feeling a certain way, right? Did you know that it wasn't until recently that trauma was recognized as being common? Only when a landmark study in 1995 revealed that 61 percent of American men and 51 percent of American women had experienced trauma did mental health professionals stop defining "trauma" as an event "outside the range of usual human experience." This means that it is normal for people to experience trauma. Talking about it openly or publicly can help.

Take Kim. Kim switched departments and went from being one of many Black women in her division to the only one in the entire department. She felt as though her internal negotiations with the people who reported to her were always laced with microaggressions and bias toward her. She talked to her boss, an older white man, about it, but he didn't understand what she was talking about. She decided to reach out to Human Resources to see if there was an employee resource group (ERG) or another type of affinity group that she could join. Kim had been at the company for six years, but because in her previous role she had been surrounded by people of color, she could not recall experiencing microaggressions and bias. Therefore, ERGs and affinity groups were not on her radar. HR informed Kim that there was an affinity group. They met monthly and the next meeting was coming up in less than a week. Kim went to the meeting and immediately found the support she was looking for. She encountered understanding and empathy, but most important, she discovered that she was not alone. She was validated, she felt seen and heard, and her feelings of isolation subsided.

My advice to you is to find a group, and if there is no group and you want to talk, then start one. If you want to take a more one-on-one approach, one idea is to identify a supportive person within your circle and talk to that person, whether they are family, a friend, or a colleague.

Sometimes even a random stranger can provide support. Once I found solace talking to a man who came to fix my windshield after a rock hit it in Badlands National Park. Joe asked what brought me to South Dakota. Before I knew it, I found myself telling this stranger how I had taken my sons on a road trip post–George Floyd to show them that this *was* their country and that they belonged here just like everyone else. Taking a road trip straight into middle America with two Black kids in the late summer of 2020 with the backdrop of the pandemic, the racial reckoning that followed George Floyd, and an upcoming presidential election was a lot. Not to mention that my boys and I just happened to be in Kenosha, Wisconsin, on August 23, 2020, the date that Jacob Blake was shot seven times by a Kenosha police officer, nearly three months to the day after George Floyd was killed. By the time we got to South Dakota, all the emotions were bubbling up. Jacob Blake's shooting had triggered me afresh. Joe listened, mainly because he was a captive audience, waiting for the windshield glass to dry. But it felt cathartic being able to say all those things to someone I was probably never going to see again.

Right before I left on the road trip, I recommended one of the negotiations that I had rescheduled the day that I saw the George Floyd video. The lawyer on the other side happened to also be a Black woman, Monique. I started the call by thanking her for being amenable to rescheduling the prior call. Monique and I had interacted on other matters before, but we never discussed anything other than deal terms—in other words, we always kept it professional. I had conducted my due diligence on her previously, and aside from both being Black women, I don't think we had anything else in common. Until that call, that is. Monique broke character for a moment and sighed. She then said, "Honestly, I was happy you sent that message because I needed a break, too. Sometimes, it's just too much . . . Too many names to list. Too many times. When will this end?" That's all she said. And you know what, she didn't have to say anything else because I understood what she meant. In that moment, I felt like I saw another side of Monique the negotiator and realized that we had more in common than met the eye.

Sometimes, as we've discussed throughout this book, it's important to seek common ground to find support and extract what you need.

Make Sense of What Happened

In the long run, I needed time to process what happened to George Floyd, but I also needed to make sense of what was happening to me. Processing is how we make sense of what is going on. Talking about what happened was helpful. I also found writing in my journal about what I was feeling and what I was observing in the state of the world helped release the thoughts I had in my mind that I did not want to share aloud with other people. I am willing to bet that you have some thoughts like that, too.

Talking and writing about what happened helped me realize that I was more than the trauma that was happening to me. Trauma can have a colossal impact on your life. In psychology, when people define themselves in relation to their trauma, it is called event centrality. Event centrality is the extent that you consider traumatic events to be integral to your life. We all know people who orient their life and their identities based on some traumatic experience (or other life-changing event, because trauma signifies a negative event). People say things like "before Mom died," or "after his surgery," or "before the accident." For me, it was "after the George Floyd murder."

A study from UNC Charlotte discovered that centrality could be both a good and a bad thing, depending on how the person moved forward. When trauma is your only story and takes over your identity, it is bad for you. And as we've seen, trauma is inextricably linked to our triggers. When someone calls us "angry Black men" or "angry Black women," perhaps what they are really seeing is the trauma seeping out. The frustration, the powerlessness, the loss of dignity, the humiliation. Remember what I said earlier about looking under the anger for the why? Acknowledge your trauma, but do not let trauma take over your identity. Make sense of what's happening. Process it. Then move on. You are more than your trauma. Use these lessons to fuel your real-life negotiations.

MAKE MEANING

When you experience a traumatic or extremely triggering event, you have the opportunity for introspection. To grow. To learn. To evolve. When bad things happen, one positive outcome is that we reevaluate what is important to us. What we can live with and whom we cannot live without. Following a traumatic event, you may decide that maybe something that you love to do is no longer what you want to do, and maybe, just maybe, you have a higher calling. Maybe you realize that there is something else that you are supposed to do with your time, your energy, and your resources. Or that there is a better way for you to live and to give back. Maybe before you were a prosecutor and you become a defense attorney or vice versa. Maybe you support more causes that reflect your values.

What are ways to make meaning? Here are some questions to ask yourself:

"What do I want my story to be?"

"How can I use my story to help others?"

"What do I want people to remember me for?"

"What's my legacy?"

In every negotiation, I want to show up as me with all my fabulousness and all my flaws and still negotiate to win every time. I want to control the narrative and not be thwarted or put off my game by things that I could have prepared for in advance by, among other things, knowing how to react when I face my kryptonite. And you know what? I want the same for you.

By the time I finally made my decision on what to do after George Floyd was killed, I knew it was 100 percent up to me. I would not succumb to pressure to be a people pleaser and just say yes to one or both sides. I was at the crossroads of different aspects of my identity and my intersectionality, and I knew that the decision was ultimately mine to make and on my timeline. I had taken the time I needed—and acknowledged my emotions and triggers.

I decided to write this book. It felt like the best way to make the long-term contribution I wanted to make.

I started to write because I wanted to help people, even in the highest-conflict situations, find successful pathways to resolution. As I continued to write, I realized I wanted to recognize people who had been left out of the narrative in other negotiation books. I wanted to normalize all the thoughts, feelings, and experiences that you have had and to validate them, and you.

I am sure that as you come to the end of this chapter, you are wondering whom I chose to stand with. The police or Black people. Do I bleed blue, or do I bleed black?

Well, the answer is simple, and you probably could have guessed it all along.

I wrote this book because I stand with you.

NEGOTIATION IRL TOOL KIT

- Protect your peace in negotiations. You can't manage others or the situation, but you can manage yourself.
- Take a step back when triggered. Remove yourself from the situation and put space and time in between you and the triggering event, especially if you feel flooded.
- Acknowledge your emotions. Identify how you are feeling to position yourself to release your negative emotions and proceed.
- Know your kryptonite. Identify your triggers and why what happened upset you. Pay attention to what sets you off and your feelings and emotions before, during, and after the triggering event.
- Regulate your emotions. Put enough space between feeling the emotion and reacting to the emotion by using cognitive reappraisal and attention control.
- Talk about your trauma. Share your story: to find support, to get a reality check, to make sense of what happened, and/or to realize that you are more than the trauma.
- Choose what you value. Make your own meaning after a traumatic event.

Conclusion

I set out to accomplish two overarching goals when I wrote this book. One, I wanted to write a book that provided tools for everyday negotiations for everyone. Two, I wanted to acknowledge that negotiation is not the same for everyone. The reality is that some negotiations and certain negotiators require customized tools.

I wrote this book because globally people were seeking more tools to learn how to negotiate in their real life.

I wrote this book because I believe that things can improve during my lifetime and that I could make the world a better place for my sons.

I wrote this book to inspire other people to share their gifts and experiences with the world so that the literature reflects the melting pot of diversity and not just a plain-vanilla approach to negotiations.

It was at the beginning of the pandemic that I finally started putting my ideas into a cohesive format that formed the basis of my book proposal. All these books were coming out exploring topics that had never been explored before in a way that was inspiring to me. I wanted to do my part. At Howard University School of Law, we learn during our first year of law school the inspiring words of famous alumnus Charles Hamilton Houston that "a lawyer is either a social engineer or a parasite on society." I am a social engineer. A social engineer is a person who affects social change and makes a positive contribution to society.

I am giving you real-life tool kits to negotiate real-life situations that involve implicit bias. Explicit bias is, well, explicit. You can see it. Implicit bias is far more scary than explicit bias because the person who holds it (which is all of us, by the way) is unaware of it and how it affects them and others on so many levels. Implicit bias is so common that we may not even pick up on it when it is reflected back at us in the mirror or staring at us on the page.

Recall the story in chapter 5 about the angry stranger. Describe him to me. What was his race? Ethnicity? How old do you think he was? I intentionally described him as having an accent and likely from another country, but I did not share his race or ethnicity. I am willing to bet that you can see him as clear as day in your mind. How did your implicit bias fill in the blanks about his description?

However you identify and reflect your intersectionality, you are a negotiator and you will negotiate every day in some form or fashion. I want you to be confident. Show them who you are. Incorporate the tools in your Negotiation IRL Tool Kit.

We need this book.

In the future, I hope that a book on straight negotiating will be enough. In the meantime, this book will help you negotiate to win. To negotiate to be who you are and get what you want even when you have been underestimated. To negotiate while Black, white, Native, Latinx, Asian, Middle Eastern, female, male, or as a member of the LGBTQIA+ family. There is space for everyone at the negotiations table. Pull up a seat. You are a negotiator, and you've got this!

Acknowledgments

To my husband and soulmate, Chad Peterman, thank you for being a true partner in all aspects of my life. Without you, there would be no book. Thank you for your constant encouragement, loving commitment, steadfast support, and unwavering belief in me. Thank you for always pushing me to go further, do more, and be better. I can do anything with you by my side.

To my sons, Chase and Cole, thank you for giving me purpose and endless laughs, hugs, and love. Thank you for understanding when I had to divide my time and miss more activities with you than I would have liked during this process. You have made me better, stronger, and more fulfilled than I could have ever imagined. Everything that I have done and continue to do is for you.

To Andrea Saavedra and Mark Tavani, thank you for being the first two people outside of my family to believe in this book and to put me on the path to drafting my proposal. Mark, thank you for answering all my book questions and for always being available to ideate and push me.

To Kathleen Murray (and to Cari Sommer for the introduction!), thank you for the insight, enthusiasm, and support. I am grateful that you helped me concretize my proposal.

To my literary agent, Gillian MacKenzie (and to Jennifer Lupo for the introduction!), I cannot thank you enough for reviewing my proposal and for seeing the potential in my ideas. Thank you for working hard to get my book in the hands of all the right editors in not one but two auctions. I could not ask for a better literary agent. I look forward to continuing to work together.

To my editor at Penguin Random House, Michelle Howry, your brilliance, enthusiasm, and knowledge are infused throughout this book. Thank you for believing in me and always making me feel as if this book was going to make a difference in the lives of many. I hope this book will do just that. Also at Putnam, I am grateful to Ivan Held, Sally Kim, Ashley McClay, Alexis Welby, and Ashley Di Dio for seeing the potential in my proposal. I'd also like to thank Heather Rodino, Andrea Peabbles, and Janine Barlow for their tireless work on this project. I also appreciate my corporate marketing team—Allison Rich, Zehra Kayi, and Racheal Periello Henry—for taking over my social media and teaching me how to reach the hearts and minds of many.

To my external editor, Dedi Felman, thank you for your directness, support, and unmatched skills. With you I felt like I had a coach who was in the trenches with me, which is invaluable for a first-time author. Thank you for making me feel that both me and my book were high priorities for you. I am eternally grateful for your coaching and guidance.

To my readers Homer LaRue, William Monning, Vanessa Kaye Watson, Chrystal Dyer LaRoche, Dawn Baker Miller, Cari Sommer, and Kayla Strauss, thank you for your honest and insightful feedback, often complying with tight turnaround times. I asked the busiest people in the world to take on the additional task of reviewing my drafts, and they came through time and time again. Additional thanks to Kayla Strauss for also assisting me with research and fact-checking. Kayla, you are such a joy to work with. I am so grateful that you made time in your busy schedule to help me while practicing law full time and being an adjunct professor.

To my executive assistant, Essence Clark, thank you for holding down the fort at BreakthroughADR so that I could focus on the book. You were understanding, thoughtful, and helpful throughout the entire process. I could not ask for a better supporter and friend.

I began and concluded my writing process in Guatemala, one of my favorite countries in the world. My heartfelt thanks to the people whom I consider to be my Guatemalan family: Ariela, Andrew, Dina, Mario, María Dolores, and Franklin. I can never repay you for opening your hearts, homes, offices, and lives to my family and me. Thank you for providing me with the perfect writing environment.

To my family and friends who listened to me wax poetic when the concept for this book could no longer live only inside my head, to all those who said something kind to me as I tried to find the right balance, and finally to everyone who understood when the writing process took over my life, leaving no time for me to fulfill other commitments, I say thank you.

Notes

Chapter 1: Negotiation Isn't the Same for Everyone

3   **Secrets from top-selling negotiation books:** Roger Fisher, William
     Ury, and Bruce Patton, *Getting to Yes*, 3rd ed. (New York: Penguin
     Putnam, 2011); William Ury, *Getting Past No* (New York: Bantam Dell,
     2007); Alexandra Carter, *Ask for More: 10 Questions to Negotiate
     Anything* (New York: Simon & Schuster, 2020); Chris Voss and Tahl
     Raz, *Never Split the Difference* (New York: HarperCollins, 2016).

6   **Negotiate in a similar manner for a new car:** Ian Ayres, "Fair Driving:
     Gender and Race Discrimination in Retail Car Negotiations," Yale
     Faculty Scholarship Series Paper (1991), paper 1540.

7   **Adopt a "late-night FM DJ" voice:** Voss, *Never Split the Difference*,
     31–33.

7   **Stereotypes of the "oversexualized" jezebel:** Seanna Leath, Morgan
     C. Jerald, Tiani Perkins, and Martinique Karee Jones, "A Qualitative
     Exploration of Jezebel Stereotype Endorsement and Sexual Behaviors
     Among Black College Women," *Journal of Black Psychology* 47, no. 4–5
     (2021): 244–83, https://doi.org/10.1177/0095798421997215.

7   **Using "negotiation jujitsu":** Fisher, *Getting to Yes*, 109–30.

8   **Undervalued their home based on their race:** Vanessa Romo, "Black
     Couple Settles Lawsuit Claiming Their Home Appraisal Was

Lowballed Due to Bias," NPR, March 9, 2023, https://www.npr.org
/2023/03/09/1162103286/home-appraisal-racial-bias-Black
-homeowners-lawsuit.

11 **"all skinfolk ain't kinfolk":** Leath, Jerald, Perkins, and Jones, "A
Qualitative Exploration of Jezebel Stereotype Endorsement and Sexual
Behaviors Among Black College Women."

Chapter 2: The Foundational Five Elements of Every Negotiation

23 **Which ruled that segregation was unconstitutional:** *Brown v. Board
of Education of Topeka*, National Archives, May 17, 1954.

29 **Universal needs that motivate individuals:** Abraham H. Maslow, "A
Theory of Human Motivation," *Psychological Review* 50 (August 2000):
370–96, http://www.livrosgratis.com.br/ler-livro-online-88633/a
-theory-of-human-motivation.

34 **Interacting with a good listener:** Dotan R. Castro, Guy Itzchakov, and
Avraham N. Kluger, "I Am Aware of My Inconsistencies but Can
Tolerate Them: The Effect of High Quality Listening on Speakers'
Attitude Ambivalence," *Personality and Social Psychology Bulletin* 43
no. 1 (January 2017): 105–20, https://journals.sagepub.com/doi/abs
/10.1177/0146167216675339.

43 **A powerful way to be personable:** Joyce E. A. Russell, "Career Coach:
The Power of Using a Name," *Washington Post*, January 12, 2014,
https://www.washingtonpost.com/business/capitalbusiness/career
-coach-the-power-of-using-a-name/2014/01/10/8ca03da0-787e-11e3
-8963-b4b654bcc9b2_story.html.

43 **"A person's name is to that person the sweetest":** Dale Carnegie, *How
to Win Friends & Influence People* (New York: Pocket Books, 1998).

Chapter 3: Show Them Who You Are

50 **Around 5 percent of venture capitalists:** "Global Women in the VC
Community," Women in VC, accessed August 6, 2023, https://www
.women-vc.com.

50 **Targeted efforts to recruit more:** "Global Women in the VC
Community."

50   **Only three individuals identified themselves as women of color:**
"Women in VC," Data from Our Global Women in VC Directory,
Women in VC, accessed June 25, 2023, https://www.women vc.com.

52   **Trust and authenticity are intertwined:** Frances X. Frei and Anne
Morriss, "Begin with Trust: The First Step to Becoming a Genuinely
Empowering Leader," *Harvard Business Review*, May–June 2020,
https://hbr.org/2020/05/begin-with-trust.

53   **Convey truthful, accurate information:** Joseph C. Nunes, Andrea
Ordanini, and Gaia Giambastiani, "The Concept of Authenticity:
What It Means to Consumers," *Journal of Marketing* 85 no. 4:
(February 2021): 1–20, https://journals.sagepub.com/doi/10.1177
/0022242921997081.

53   **People as authentic and trustworthy:** Herminia Ibarra, "The
Authenticity Paradox," *Harvard Business Review*, January–February
2015, https://hbr.org/2015/01/the-authenticity-paradox.

53   **Motivated while acting consistently:** Ibarra, "The Authenticity
Paradox."

53   **Link between integrity:** Salman Majeed, Jianping Xue, Liangbo
Zhang, and Zhimon Zhou, "Do Brand Competence and Warmth
Always Influence Purchase Intention? The Moderating Role of
Gender," *Frontiers in Psychology* 11 no. 248 (February 2020), https://
doi.org/10.3389/fpsyg.2020.00248.

53   **Successful brand like Ben & Jerry's:** Jeff Fromm, "The Purpose Series:
Ben & Jerry's Authentic Purpose," *Forbes*, June 4, 2019, https://www
.forbes.com/sites/jefffromm/2019/06/04/the-purpose-series-ben-jerrys
-authentic-purpose/?sh=f03f5975bad0.

53   **A brand that communicates:** Majeed, Xue, Zhang, and Zhou, "Do
Brand Competence and Warmth Always Influence Purchase
Intention?"

54   **Short film about a Black father:** Matthew A. Cherry, *Hair Love*,
accessed June 25, 2023, https://www.kickstarter.com/projects/matthe
wacherry/hair-love-animated-short-film.

55   **A deal for a children's book:** Joi-Marie McKenzie, "Matthew A.
Cherry Wants *Hair Love* to 'Chip Away At' Negative Stereotypes
Around Black Fathers," *Essence*, December 6, 2020, https://www
.essence.com/entertainment/only-essence/matthew-cherry-hair-love
-cover/.

55   **"Living with Black hair my whole life":** Bethonie Butler, "How *Hair
Love* Went from a Beloved Kickstarter Project to an Oscar-Nominated

Animated Short," *Washington Post*, February 3, 2020, https://www
.washingtonpost.com/arts-entertainment/2020/02/03/how-hair-love
-went-beloved-kickstarter-project-an-oscar-nominated-animated
-short/.

59   **Skincare routine of many Jamaicans:** "A Dream Fulfilled," *Jamaica
Observer*, April 11, 2021, https://www.jamaicaobserver.com/art
-culture/a-dream-fulfilled/.

65   **"Identity shapes the kinds of power":** "Conflict Coaching: Its Value in
Special Education Dispute Resolution," The Center for Appropriate
Dispute Resolution in Special Education, webinar presented January 9,
2013, https://www.cadreworks.org/resources/cadre-materials/conflict
-coaching-its-value-special-education-dispute-resolution.

65   **Conflict coaching:** Ross Brinkert and Tricia S. Jones, *Conflict
Coaching: Conflict Management Strategies and Skills for the Individual*
(Thousand Oaks: Sage Publications, 2008).

66   **Identities can be described in six categories:** Brinkert, *Conflict
Coaching.*

66   **Authenticity paradox:** Ibarra, "The Authenticity Paradox."

67   **Our stories constantly evolve:** Dan P. McAdams, "The Psychology of
Life Stories," *Northwestern University Review of General Psychology* 5
no. 2 (2001): 100–22, https://www.sesp.northwestern.edu/docs
/publications/430816076490a3ddfc3fe1.pdf.

70   **Attributes create the norms:** Ruby White Starr, "Moving from the
Mainstream to the Margins: Lessons in Culture and Power," *Springer
Journal of Family Violence* 33 no. 8 (August 31, 2018): 551–57, https://
doi.org/10.1007%2Fs10896-018-9984-1.

72   **High school student Andrew Johnson:** Roman Stubbs, "A Wrestler
Was Forced to Cut His Dreadlocks Before a Match. His Town Is Still
Looking for Answers," *Washington Post*, June 4, 2019, https://www
.washingtonpost.com/sports/2019/04/17/wrestler-was-forced-cut-his
-dreadlocks-before-match-his-town-is-still-looking-answers/.

72   **White female referee cutting his locks:** Stubbs, "A Wrestler Was
Forced to Cut His Dreadlocks Before a Match."

72   **Banned by the school district:** Chelsea Cox, "Texas Teen Banned by
High School from Attending Graduation After Refusing to Cut
Dreadlocks," *USA Today*, January 24, 2020, https://www.usatoday.com
/story/news/nation/2020/01/24/black-texas-teen-barred-high-school
-after-graduation-not-cutting-dreadlocks/4562210002/.

72   **Black hairstyles have been censured:** Jonathan Stempel, "FedEx Seeks to Void $366 Mln Verdict for Black Former Worker Who Alleged Bias," Reuters, November 1, 2022, https://www.reuters.com/legal/fedex-seeks-void-366-mln-verdict-black-former-worker-who-alleged-bias-2022-11-01/; Howard Henderson and Jennifer Wyatt Bourgeois, "Penalizing Black Hair in the Name of Academic Success Is Undeniably Racist, Unfounded, and Against the Law," Brookings, February 23, 2021, https://www.brookings.edu/blog/how-we-rise/2021/02/23/penalizing-black-hair-in-the-name-of-academic-success-is-undeniably-racist-unfounded-and-against-the-law/; Adina Campbell, "Afro Hair School Bans Probably Illegal, Says Watchdog," BBC News, October 27, 2022, https://www.bbc.com/news/education-63402905.

73   **CROWN stands for:** "The CROWN Act," Legal Defense Fund, accessed June 25, 2023, https://www.naacpldf.org/crown-act/.

73   **Twenty-two states:** "The CROWN Act."

74   **Who fought for the CROWN Act:** "About the CROWN Act," Legal Defense Fund, accessed June 25, 2023, https://www.thecrownact.com/about.

Chapter 4: Peek Inside Their Bag

80   **Incomplete information about a counterpart:** Peter C. Cramton, "The Role of Time and Information in Bargaining" Stanford Graduate School of Business (1984), working paper 729, https://www.gsb.stanford.edu/faculty-research/working-papers/role-time-information-bargaining.

81   **Universities look at these accounts:** Josh Moody, "Why Colleges Look at Students' Social Media," *US News*, August 22, 2019, https://www.usnews.com/education/best-colleges/articles/2019-08-22/why-colleges-look-at-students-social-media-accounts.

81   **Companies screen social media:** David Cotriss, "Keep It Clean: Social Media Screenings Gain in Popularity," *Business News Daily,* May 11, 2023, https://www.businessnewsdaily.com/2377-social-media-hiring.html.

93   **Cannabis industry in New York:** *Estimated Tax Revenues from Marijuana Legalization in New York,* New York City Comptroller Report, May 15, 2018, accessed June 25, 2023, https://comptroller.nyc

.gov/reports/estimated-tax-revenues-from-marijuana-legalization-in
-new-york/.

Chapter 5: Be Heard in the Face of Implicit Bias

107   **"Scientific knowledge about bias and disparities":** "About Us,"
Project Implicit, accessed June 25, 2020, https://implicit.harvard.edu
/implicit/takeatest.html.

107   **Implicit Association Test:** Betsy Mason, "Making People Aware of
Their Implicit Biases Doesn't Usually Change Minds. But Here's What
Does Work," PBS News, June 10, 2020, https://www.pbs.org/newshour
/nation/making-people-aware-of-their-implicit-biases-doesnt-usually
-change-minds-but-heres-what-does-work.

Chapter 6: Recovering from Unintended Offense

134   **George Floyd's murder in the US:** Evan Hill, Ainara Tiefenthäler,
Christiaan Triebert, Drew Jordan, Haley Willis, and Robin Stein,
"How George Floyd Was Killed in Police Custody," *New York Times*,
published May 31, 2020, https://www.nytimes.com/2020/05/31/us
/george-floyd-investigation.html.

134   **White people asked themselves:** Savala Nolan, "Black and Brown
People Have Been Protesting for Centuries. It's White People Who Are
Responsible for What Happens Next," *Time*, June 1, 2020, https://time
.com/5846072/black-people-protesting-white-people-responsible-what
-happens-next/.

134   *White Fragility* **and** *How to Be an Antiracist*: Heather Schwedel,
"There's Been a Run on Anti-racist Books," *Slate*, June 1, 2020, https://
slate.com/culture/2020/06/antiracist-books-sold-out-amazon-george
-floyd-protests.html.

136   **Dr. Paul Ekman defines "hot spots":** Paul Ekman and Wallace V.
Friesen, *Unmasking the Face: A Guide to Recognizing Emotions from
Facial Clues* (Los Altos: Malor Books, 2003).

138   **Emotions can impact one's physical environment:** Jasper H. B. de
Groot, Maarten J. A. Duijndam, Annemarie Kaldewaij, et al.,
"Chemosignals Communicate Human Emotions," *Psychological Science*
23 no. 11 (2012): 1417–24, https://doi.org/10.1177/0956797612445317.

138   **Has a scientific basis in chemical signals:** Heidi Moawad, "How Real Are Vibes: The Good and the Bad?," *Neurology Live*, February 15, 2018, https://www.neurologylive.com/view/how-real-are-vibes-good-and -bad.

148   **Trust can be reestablished:** Lily Zheng, "Enough with the Corporate Non-Apologies for DEI-Related Harm," *Harvard Business Review*, April 15, 2022, https://hbr.org/2022/04/enough-with-the-corporate -non-apologies-for-dei-related-harm.

148   **If the person who committed the offense apologizes:** Maurice Schweitzer, John Hershey, and Eric Bradlow, "Promises and Lies: Restoring Violated Trust," *Organizational Behavior and Human Decision Processes* 101 (2006): 1–19, https://doi.org/10.1016/j.obhdp .2006.05.005.

149   **Relationships can be improved by increased forgiveness:** Frederic Luskin and Carl E. Thoresen, "Stanford Forgiveness Project," Hawaii Forgiveness Project, accessed August 7, 2023, http://www.hawaii forgivenessproject.org/Stanford.htm.

149   **It may be especially hard for BIPOC:** Gillian White, "Black Workers Really Do Need to Be Twice as Good," *The Atlantic*, October 7, 2015, https://www.theatlantic.com/business/archive/2015/10/why-black -workers-really-do-need-to-be-twice-as-good/409276/.

Chapter 7: Negotiating When You're the Target

160   **"Prepping your children":** Gustavo Solis, "For Black Parents, 'The Talk' Binds Generations and Reflects Changes in America," USC News, March 10, 2021, https://news.usc.edu/183102/the-talk-usc-Black -parents-children-racism-america/.

161   **Collective trauma:** Ayesha Rascoe, "How Black People Can Cope with the Trauma of Witnessing Repeated Death and Violence Against Them," NPR, January 29, 2023, https://www.npr.org/2023/01/29 /1152387220/how-black-people-can-cope-with-the-trauma-of -witnessing-repeated-death-and-viole.

163   **A nonviolent sit-in:** "Greensboro Lunch Counter Sit-In," Library of Congress, accessed August 8, 2023, https://www.loc.gov/exhibits /odyssey/educate/lunch.html.

163   **Subjecting themselves to simulations:** "Greensboro Lunch Counter Sit-in."

167   **"Bad apples":** Chris Rock, *Tamborine*, Netflix, 2018, https://netflix
      .com/title/80167498.

168   **Controlling your breathing:** Emma Seppala, Christina Cradley, and
      Michael R. Goldstein, "Research: Why Breathing Is So Effective at
      Reducing Stress," *Harvard Business Review*, September 29, 2020,
      https://hbr.org/2020/09/research-why-breathing-is-so-effective-at
      -reducing-stress.

168   **Hold it for four seconds:** Gary Holl, Manuela M. Kogon, et al., "Brief
      Structured Respiration Practices Enhance Mood and Reduce
      Physiological Arousal," *Cell Reports Medicine* 4 no. 1 (January 2023):
      100895, https://doi.org/10.1016/j.xcrm.2022.100895.

169   **It focuses the mind:** Jenna Fletcher, "How to Use 4-7-8 Breathing for
      Anxiety," *Medical News Today*, January 11, 2023, https://www
      .medicalnewstoday.com/articles/324417#how-to-do-it.

169   **Remain present and concentrate:** Emma Loewe, "How to Use the Box
      Breath to Call in Calm & Focus On Demand," *Mind Body Green*, July
      6, 2022, https://www.mindbodygreen.com/articles/box-breathing.

169   **Breathing can reduce anxiety:** Johanna Abendroth, Thomas Jacobsen,
      Stefan Rottger, Dominique A. Theobald, "The Effectiveness of Combat
      Tactical Breathing as Compared with Prolonged Exhalation," *Applied
      Psychophysiology Biofeedback* 46 no. 1 (March 2021): 19–28, https://doi
      .org/10.1007/s10484-020-09485-w.

171   **Decluttering your environment helps your brain:** Diane Roberts
      Stoler, "The Many Mental Benefits of Decluttering," *Psychology Today*,
      February 15, 2023, https://www.psychologytoday.com/us/blog
      /the-resilient-brain/202302/the-many-mental-benefits-of-decluttering.

171   **Alleviate mental stress:** Jo Barton and Mike Rogerson, "The
      Importance of Greenspace for Mental Health," *BJPsych International*
      14 no. 4 (November 2017): 79–81, https://www.ncbi.nlm.nih.gov/pmc
      /articles/PMC5663018/.

171   **Pattern interruptions:** Patricia Duchene, "The Science Behind Pattern
      Interrupt," *Forbes*, July 17, 2020, https://www.forbes.com/sites
      /patriciaduchene/2020/07/17/the-science-behind-pattern-interrupt/?
      sh=7ddaadc04207.

171   **Self-reflect, and process:** Jennifer Porter, "Why You Should Make
      Time for Self-Reflection (Even If You Hate Doing It)," *Harvard Business
      Review*, March 21, 2017, https://hbr.org/2017/03/why-you-should-make
      -time-for-self-reflection-even-if-you-hate-doing-it.

172   **Cognitive reappraisal:** Anna Brunner, Rachel Friedman, Markera C. Jones, Amanda J. Shallcross, and Allison S. Troy, "Cognitive Reappraisal and Acceptance: Effects on Emotion, Physiology, and Perceived Cognitive Costs," *Emotion*, 18 no. 1 (February 2018): 58–74, https://doi.org/10.1037/emo0000371.

179   **In her book *The Light We Carry*:** Michelle Obama, *The Light We Carry* (New York: Crown Publishing, 2022).

Chapter 8: Know Your Kryptonite

184   **Unarmed Black men and women:** Alia Chugtai, "Know Their Names: Black People Killed by the Police in the U.S. 2020," Al Jazeera, accessed August 7, 2023, https://interactive.aljazeera.com/aje/2020/know-their -names/index.html.

186   **"Go to the balcony":** William Ury, *Getting Past No* (New York: Bantam Books, 1991).

188   **Psychological impact of Floyd's death:** Johannes C. Eichstaedt, Garrick T. Sherman, Salvatore Giorgi, Steven O. Roberts, Megan E. Reynolds, Lyle H. Ungar, Sharath Chandra Guntuku, "The Emotional and Mental Health Impact of the Murder of George Floyd on the US Population," *Proceedings of the National Academy of Sciences* 118 no. 39 (September 2021), https://doi.org/10.1073/pnas.2109139118; erratum in: *Proceedings of the National Academy of Sciences* 118 no. 47 (November 2021).

189   **Emotions impact the negotiation process:** Kimberlyn Leary, Julianna Pillemer, and Michael Wheeler, "Negotiating with Emotion," *Harvard Business Review*, January–February 2013, https://hbr.org/2013/01 /negotiating-with-emotion.

190   **Understanding your emotions:** "Emotion Focused Therapy," Good Therapy, accessed August 7, 2023, https://www.goodtherapy.org/learn -about-therapy/types/emotion-focused-therapy.

194   **Feelings go away:** Nedra Glover Tawwab, *Set Boundaries, Find Peace* (New York: TarcherPerigee, 2021); Nedra Glover Tawwab, "The Question I'm Asked Most as a Therapist—and My Answer," Shine, November 9, 2020, https://advice.theshineapp.com/articles /the-question-im-asked-most-as-a-therapist-and-my -answer/.

198 **Neural mechanisms can help you downregulate:** Patrick Sweeney and Yunlei Yang, "Neural Circuit Mechanisms Underlying Emotional Regulation of Homeostatic Feeding," *Trends in Endocrinology and Metabolism* 28 no. 6 (June 2017): 437–48, https://doi.org/10.1016/j.tem.2017.02.006.

199 **Ways to practice emotional regulation:** Jacob Aday, Will Rizer, and Joshua M. Carlson, "Chapter 2—Neural Mechanisms of Emotions and Affect," in *Emotions and Affect in Human Factors and Human-Computer Interaction*, ed. Myounghoon Jeon (London): Academic Press, 2017), 27–87.

200 **Pain and diverting someone's attention:** Wallace E. Dixon Jr., Brenda J. Salley, and Andrea D. Clements, "Temperament, Distraction, and Learning in Toddlerhood," *Infant Behavior and Development* 29 no. 3 (July 2006): 342–57, https://doi.org/10.1016/j.infbeh.2006.01.002.

203 **A landmark study:** Ellen Hendriksen, "5 Reasons to Talk About Trauma," *Psychology Today*, March 27, 2019, https://www.psychologytoday.com/intl/blog/how-be-yourself/201903/5-reasons-talk-about-trauma.

206 **A study from UNC Charlotte:** Jessica M. Groleau, Lawrence G. Calhoun, Arnie Cann, and Richard Tedeschi "The Role of Centrality of Events in Posttraumatic Distress and Posttraumatic Growth," *Psychological Trauma: Theory, Research, Practice, and Policy* 5 no. 5 (2013): 477–83, https://doi.org/10.1037/a0028809.

Index